#1 *New York Times* Bestselling Author

RICHARD EYRE

TENNIS

AND

LIFE

30 WINNING LESSONS FOR THE TWO MOST TIMELESS GAMES

FAMILIUS

Familius books are available at special discounts for bulk purchases, whether for sales promotions or for family or corporate use. For more information, contact Familius Sales at 559-876-2170 or email orders@familius.com.

Library of Congress Cataloging-in-Publication Data
2015955951
ISBN 9781942934448

Edited by Lindsay Sandberg
Cover and book design by David Miles
Photography credit: Shutterstock.com

10 9 8 7 6 5 4 3 2 1
First Edition
Printed in China

*Written for people who
play either game . . . but
particularly for those who
play both.*

Life is best understood through metaphors.

So is tennis.

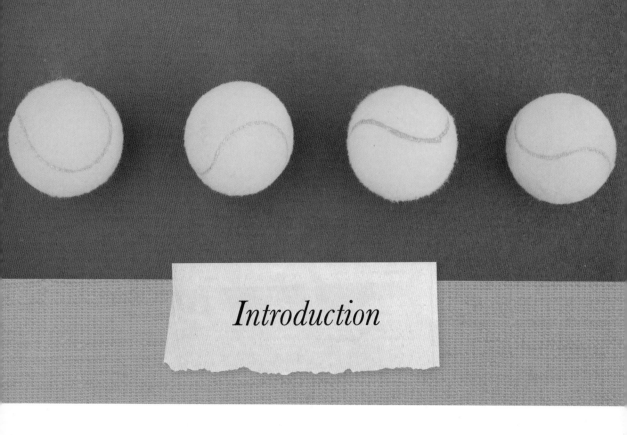

Introduction

TWO GAMES

I hope there will not be too much resentment toward my calling life a game. Games are made up of structured but unpredictable situations, with rules and variables and competition, and they produce wins and losses and sometimes ties. The description fits *life* at least as well as it fits *tennis*.

Our success (and our happiness) in both games depends greatly on our awareness and our attitudes, because each is largely entwined with the psychological. This is a book on how to alter our perspective and thus improve our performance in both games.

The book springs from my own experience on the court and in the world . . . and from my observation that my ups and downs in tennis seem in many ways to mirror and even to correspond with my ups and downs in life.

PERSPECTIVE

Ultimately, this book is centered on parallels and perspectives.

A new perspective is a new way of seeing, which can result in a new, better way of doing. Sometimes, the change of mind and heart brought about by a new perspective can be quick and dramatic. Case in point: a large ship's radar showed it on a collision course with another vessel, so the captain radioed the other ship, demanding that it change course. But the reply came back, "No, you change course." Angered, the captain answered, "I am a large mega-tanker; you change course immediately." The perspective-changing reply came back, "I am a lighthouse; *you* change course!"

When we see things more accurately or gain a clearer idea of what is happening, we usually make the right decisions and the correct adjustments. Parallels or comparisons sometimes aid perspective, and metaphors can become the starting point for improvement and for enjoyment, which are the two things most of us want from tennis and from life.

SUBTITLES

Several subtitles were considered for this book. Rather than throwing the rejects away, they are listed here as a kind of an introduction to the introduction.

Tennis and Life:

- *Thirty Approaches to a Better Attitude in Both Games*
- *Some Keys to Happiness on the Court and in the World*
- *How to Keep From Smashing Your Racket in Both Games*
- *Winning Attitudes That Apply to Both*
- *How Playing One Can Help You Play the Other*
- *Tennis as a Metaphor for Life; Life as a Metaphor for Tennis*
- *Making Your Mind Work for You in Both Games*
- *Mind Games to Help You Win at Both*

You get the idea.

THE LANGUAGE

No other game mirrors life as accurately as tennis. Even the terminology of tennis parallels many of the most pivotal and defining words of life.

- Love
- Faults
- Serve
- Receive
- Winners
- Advantage

- Return
- Unforced error
- Breaks
- Holds
- Challenges
- On the line

What a game.
What a metaphor.
What a way to look at life.

LEVELS OF LOVING THE GAME

My first level of appreciation for Tennis
Was that it paid my way through college.
I had come to play basketball,
    but that took four hours a day, all year.
The tennis team, at least at that school, in that era,
    was just March, April, and May.
Relaxed, easy practices and great early-spring road trips
    to warmer places.
The scholarships were equal. I switched.

My second level of appreciation for the game
Was in an early and busy career stage
When I realized I could play for an hour at noon
    instead of eating lunch
And lose weight and tension at the same time.

Level three of my tennis obsession came
When we lived in London and I fell in love
    with Wimbledon and grass courts
And quick trips across the channel to the red clay of
    Roland-Garros.
And the first week of the majors where one can walk
    around
And look for drama, tiebreakers, and fifth sets.

Level four was when basketball had become
  too dangerous for my knees
And tennis had become a family activity.
We built a court, and tennis was part
  of every family reunion and gathering.

Level five came when I played
  in a national 50s age group tournament
At a California location that was also hosting the 90s,
  which had a full 32 draw.
The tournament referee noticed that 4 of the 32 were 95,
And for the first time, the USTA created a 95-and-over
  singles division.
I watched the final—two 95-year-olds
  who could still get around, still play.
I congratulated the winner and told him
  how awesome it was
That he could still hit the ball.
"Hell," he said, "hitting it is not the problem;
It's picking the damn thing up that hurts!"
I thought, *I'm playing in my fifties! I have another*
  forty-five years of tennis!

Level six developed gradually, as I thought about,
Over many years,
How remarkably similar tennis is to life.

BOTH

Chicken or egg? People who have read this book ask:
"How did you go about writing it?
Did you think of a life principle first
And then look for a parallel in tennis?
Or did you notice something while playing tennis
That seemed to apply to life?"
Both!

The arrow points both ways.
And there is also a second double-headed arrow
That points back and forth
Between cause and effect.
It is the arrow of skill and joy.
Do people learn to play tennis better and thus enjoy it more
Or do they learn to enjoy it more and thus play better?
Both!

The same questions applied to life would have the same answer.
The arrow points both ways.
Do we learn how to live and thus love life more
Or do we learn to love and thus get better at life?
Both!

What is the hope—and the goal—of this book?
Is it to help you enjoy more or to win more?
Both!

Contents

II. DOUBLES

After Match and Aftermath: A Simple Suggestion for Implementation:
Implementation by Conscious Concentration and by Subconscious Self-Programming

Warming Up: A Dozen Unique Ways in Which Tennis Mirrors Life

WARMING TO THE NOTION OF A NEW KIND OF SELF-HELP

Before you get into a tough match, you need to be fully warmed up. Before you get into this book, you need to be fully tuned in to the concept of using tennis as a metaphor for life (and vice versa).

Any good player will tell you that the game of tennis is mostly mental. On the professional level, it is the *mind* that separates great players from good ones, and at the recreational level, it's what happens inside—your confidence and your attitude—that determines what happens outside in the match.

Any psychologist (or philosopher, or priest, or private citizen, for that matter) will tell you that success in life is also primarily a product of attitude.

And this book will tell you that the two games can work as good metaphors (and good training grounds) for each other . . . and that certain principles can be better understood (and better applied) when thought of in terms of tennis *and* in terms of everyday life.

What follows, then, is essentially a unique type of self-help book written for three kinds of people:

1. Those who want to improve their tennis—and who accept the idea that their mind affects their play as much or more than their body.
2. Those who want to improve their lives—and who agree with great teachers of all ages that life is best understood through metaphors and best lived through attitudes.
3. Those who wouldn't mind a little improvement in both games.

Readers who are "number ones" may want to read the left-hand page of each chapter first—since it deals with tennis. "Number twos" can start on the second part of each perspective—the right-hand page—which deals with life. "Number threes" can start wherever their inclination leads them.

TENNIS: THE BEST SPORTS METAPHOR FOR LIFE

All games have their devotees—even their fanatics. I know people (so do you) who live for golf, people who are addicted to running or to cycling or to swimming, people who are obsessed with football. I happen to love basketball, pretty much living it during the season—either watching or playing.

But tennis, for many of us, goes even further. Tennis is a way of thinking; tennis is a lifestyle; tennis is a paradigm. Tennis is global, international, and boundaryless. Tennis is fundamentally different from any other sport, and in each way that it is different, it is also more like life and thus a better metaphor for life.

On the following warm-up pages, consider twelve unique ways in which tennis mirrors life, and get used to the pattern of a principle of tennis being followed by a corresponding principle for life. Use one to better understand the other.

I

ONLY TENNIS IS A TRULY INDIVIDUAL SPORT

In team sports, you rise and fall along with your teammates,
And even in most "individual sports," the coach is a big part of
   the game,
Making the decisions, calling the plays,
Stopping play, controlling tempo, making adjustments.
Even in golf, the caddy might help you pick a club.
And in wrestling, the coach can yell instructions.
In tennis, it's just you.

No teammates to blame or to take the ball on a big play.
Coaches may help you practice and train and strategize,
   but they are banned
From even giving you hand signals during a match.
You're on your own; it's up to you!
On the court, at match time,
It's just you.

I

LIFE COMES DOWN TO YOU

Advice-seeking is good;
Example-following, being mentored,
Apprenticing,
Knowing where to find help
And asking for it—all good.
You may even have a whole team of helpers or coworkers,
But
When it comes to game time,
To personal-decision time,
No one else can choose for you.
You're on your own.
You draw on faith and advice,
But it's up to you.

ONLY IN TENNIS IS THERE A CONSTANT MIX OF ACTING AND REACTING

In tennis, there is more back-and-forth than in other games.
Offense and defense are more blended—less separate.
In most other games, there are distinct offenses and defenses,
Sometimes with different people playing each.
The O may leave the field while the D is doing its thing
Or run to the other end of the court and transition to D.
But in tennis, the O and the D interchange by the second.
Receiving the ball and hitting the ball are
    two sides of the same motion.
Acting and reacting are two parts of one thing.
The ball is going instantly after it is coming.
Acting and reacting switch in an instant
Or, at their best, blend smoothly into one.
A thin net and a fraction of a second is all that separates them.
On the court, at match time,
It's just you.

LIFE IS A NATURAL BLEND OF ACTING AND REACTING

"The best offense is a good defense"—sometimes.
"The best defense is a good offense"—sometimes.
But in life, they're too integrated to separate.
"Act, don't react" is a nice motto for self-control,
But outside of self, there is not much we can control.
The wisest people view acting and reacting as two sides
Of one coin,
And happiness is less a factor of what life throws at us
Than of how we handle whatever comes.

ONLY IN TENNIS DO YOU GET A SECOND CHANCE

In basketball, you might get a second free throw,
But it doesn't make up for missing the first.
In golf, you might take a mulligan,
But your playing partner might object.
In football, you get a second down,
But the ball stays where first down left it.
In bowling, you get a second roll,
But the pins from the first roll still count.
In baseball, you get another pitch or another swing,
But the ball or strike from the last one stays on the scoreboard.

Only in tennis is there a true second chance.
Everything resets after the first serve.
The missed serve doesn't matter.
You start over.
And you can readjust, realign, recalibrate,
Redo whatever the first serve missed.

IN LIFE, THERE IS ALWAYS ANOTHER OPPORTUNITY

Life continuously gives us second chances.
Every day is a new day.
For those who don't give up,
There is always another opportunity,
Another possibility.
When we learn from a mistake (or a "fault"),
We can readjust, realign, recalculate, even repent
And use the error to help us
Get it right
The next time.

ONLY IN TENNIS DO YOU MAKE THE CALLS

Assuming you are not playing at Wimbledon,
You are your own umpire and referee in tennis.
You make the calls on your side of the court for your opponent.
That is unique.
His destiny is in your hands, and he trusts you with the call.
As the match goes on, the trust builds—
Or not.
You learn the character of your opponent by his calls,
And you develop your own character by yours.

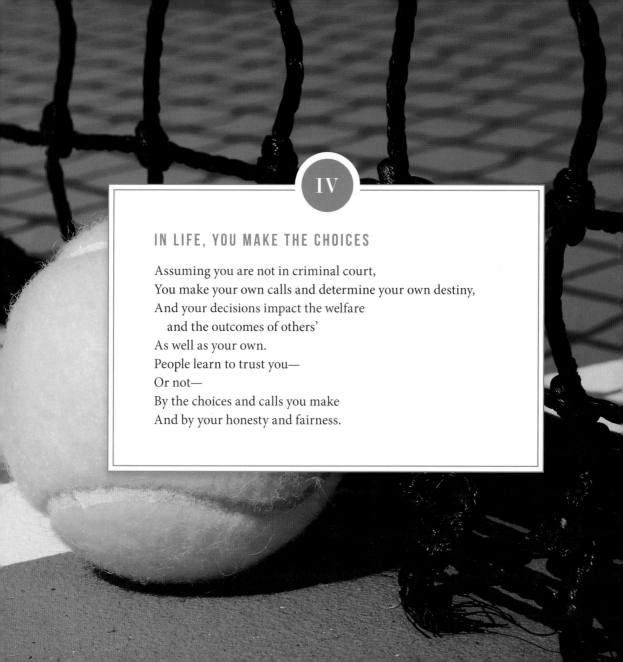

IV

IN LIFE, YOU MAKE THE CHOICES

Assuming you are not in criminal court,
You make your own calls and determine your own destiny,
And your decisions impact the welfare
   and the outcomes of others'
As well as your own.
People learn to trust you—
Or not—
By the choices and calls you make
And by your honesty and fairness.

ONLY IN TENNIS DO YOU WARM UP YOUR OPPONENT

It is not only your job to call your opponent's shots in or out—
You are also responsible for warming him up.
And he warms you up.
It's a chance to look for weaknesses
But also to complement each other's game.
You are mutually dependent as opponents.
Ultimately, one's game exists at the level of his opponent.
Tennis is like a mirror—
Each shot reflects and responds to its counterpart
And you get better only by playing better players.
You learn the character of your opponent by his calls,
And you develop your own character by yours.

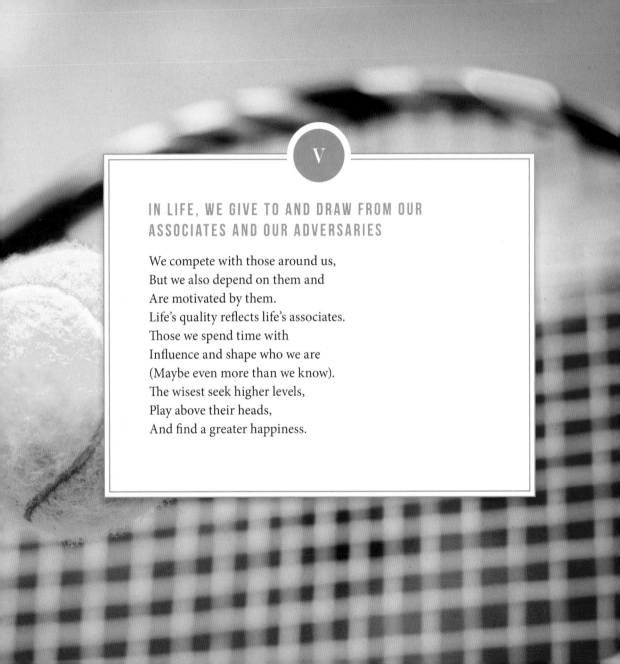

V

IN LIFE, WE GIVE TO AND DRAW FROM OUR ASSOCIATES AND OUR ADVERSARIES

We compete with those around us,
But we also depend on them and
Are motivated by them.
Life's quality reflects life's associates.
Those we spend time with
Influence and shape who we are
(Maybe even more than we know).
The wisest seek higher levels,
Play above their heads,
And find a greater happiness.

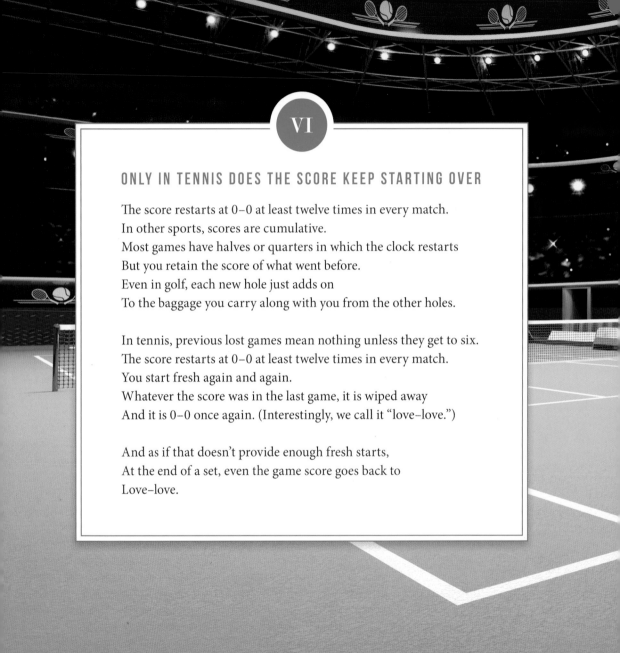

VI

ONLY IN TENNIS DOES THE SCORE KEEP STARTING OVER

The score restarts at 0–0 at least twelve times in every match.
In other sports, scores are cumulative.
Most games have halves or quarters in which the clock restarts
But you retain the score of what went before.
Even in golf, each new hole just adds on
To the baggage you carry along with you from the other holes.

In tennis, previous lost games mean nothing unless they get to six.
The score restarts at 0–0 at least twelve times in every match.
You start fresh again and again.
Whatever the score was in the last game, it is wiped away
And it is 0–0 once again. (Interestingly, we call it "love–love.")

And as if that doesn't provide enough fresh starts,
At the end of a set, even the game score goes back to
Love–love.

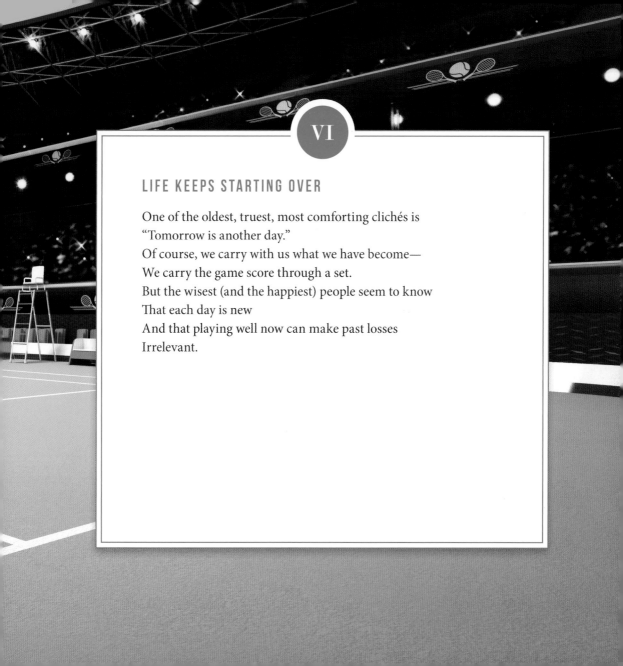

VI

LIFE KEEPS STARTING OVER

One of the oldest, truest, most comforting clichés is
"Tomorrow is another day."
Of course, we carry with us what we have become—
We carry the game score through a set.
But the wisest (and the happiest) people seem to know
That each day is new
And that playing well now can make past losses
Irrelevant.

ONLY IN TENNIS DO SOME POINTS MEAN DRAMATICALLY MORE THAN OTHERS

In most games, because they are cumulative,
One point ultimately counts the same as any other.
But in tennis, some points
   are completely valueless and inconsequential
While other single points determine the outcome.
"Point" is a more important word in tennis
Where it is
Not just an addition to the score.
A point is a defined segment
Or a section of the game—an entity,
Like an inning, or a hole, or a frame, or a half.
Key matches turn on one or two key points
Determined by a handful
Of timely and memorable shots.

LIFE CONTAINS PIVOT POINTS OF ENORMOUS IMPORTANCE

Some parts of life are fairly routine,
But now and then, moments come along
That make or break us.
Certain days, certain pivotal decisions,
Chart the direction and establish the outcome
Of our whole life.
The wisest (and the happiest)
Concentrate and consecrate
All they have on the decisions and the dimensions
That really count.

ONLY IN TENNIS ARE THERE HUGE TIME VARIABLES

Most games are governed by clocks.
The winner is the one who is ahead
When time runs out.
The clock controls the game and how you play it.
In many sports, time is the ultimate opponent—
You run or swim or ride or shoot against the clock.
Even most non-timed games—golf, billiards,
    baseball, bowling—
Operate within fairly standard time variables.
But a tennis match could last 40 minutes
Or more than 4 hours.
Each point can be very short or very long,
And the score, in tiebreakers
Or in a final non-tiebreaker set,
Is potentially limitless.

VIII

LIFE'S TIMING IS UNCERTAIN AND UNPREDICTABLE

Life can be short or long,
And its length is only partially in our control.
Even organized portions of life
   (months, weeks, years)
Can seem shorter or longer
Depending on challenge, routine, and purpose.
The wisest and the happiest among us
Try to control their time
Rather than letting it control them
And learn that a life of great ideas
And of spiritual insight
Is potentially limitless.

ONLY IN TENNIS DO VARIETY AND INVENTION PRODUCE MORE REWARDS THAN PREDICTABILITY AND CONVENTION

It's a mix in all games, of course,
Doing standard things the same—seeking perfection
While at the same time innovating and surprising,
Tactically and strategically.
But tennis is more of the latter,
A chance to surprise on every point, every stroke
A new opportunity, challenge, dilemma
Each time the ball comes at you.
Every shot can have a different angle, stroke, spin.
You take what it gives you and decide,
Very quickly,
How to handle it and how to send it back.

IX

LIFE IN TODAY'S WORLD REWARDS INDIVIDUALITY AND INNOVATION

"Envy is ignorance; imitation is suicide,"
Said Emerson.
More today than ever before,
Being able to create rather than conform
Sets one apart and above.
Ask both "Why?" and "Why not?"
And find happiness in both of
The answers.
We don't always control what comes at us,
But we do decide how we will respond
And whether to choose, in that instant,
Comfortable conformity or innovative independence.

ONLY IN TENNIS ARE THERE GAMES WITHIN GAMES WITHIN GAMES

Each shot (of which there are infinite varieties)
Finishes and
Becomes part of a point (which can be long or short, fast or slow) which
Finishes and
Becomes part of a game (which can end quickly or drag on) which
Finishes and
Becomes part of a set (which can be a rout, a tie break, or a marathon) which
Finishes and
Becomes part of a match (which can be on any surface) which
Finishes and
Becomes part of a tournament (which can be anywhere in the world) which
Finishes and
Becomes part of a season that never finishes.
So many independent, interlocking
Parts, phases, places,
Variables, variations, vacillations.
The best players love it all, big and small.

LIFE IS DIVISIBLE IN SO MANY NATURAL WAYS

Moments make hours make days make weeks
Make months make years make seasons of life.
Each time frame combines with its counterparts,
Creating its collective.
Live in the smallest moments;
Appreciate their singular reality.
Know that joy is in the present
And that bigger screens both from then and from when
Can frame the now
And give perspective to the moment.
The deliberately divided and appreciated life feels longer
And offers more.

ONLY IN TENNIS ARE THERE INFINITE WAYS TO WIN AND TO WATCH

Most games are so rule bound and single objective
That points are won in only one way.
The ball goes through the hoop
Or across the goal;
Into the net, through the uprights,
Or into the hole.

In tennis, points are won in any number of ways.
Tennis has more dimensions.
There are different lines for service and strokes;
You can hit the ball before or after it bounces;
You aim over the net, not into it—over by one inch or 50 feet.
The only requirement is to keep the ball within the lines.

There are also lots of ways to watch tennis.
At tournaments, spectators are active and selective
Not restricted to one seat or one match or one score.
Many matches go on at once; you can create your own
    agenda.
Find the most exciting, watch a little of each,
Go from one to the other in random order.

LIFE HAS SO MANY ROUTES, SO MANY WAYS

This earth is an orbiting school,
Containing infinite variety, variation, and alternatives,
All more accessible today
Than ever before.
The wise broaden rather than limit themselves,
Thrilled rather than threatened by
Diversity, differences, new dimensions,
And frequently find happiness
In the unexpected places.

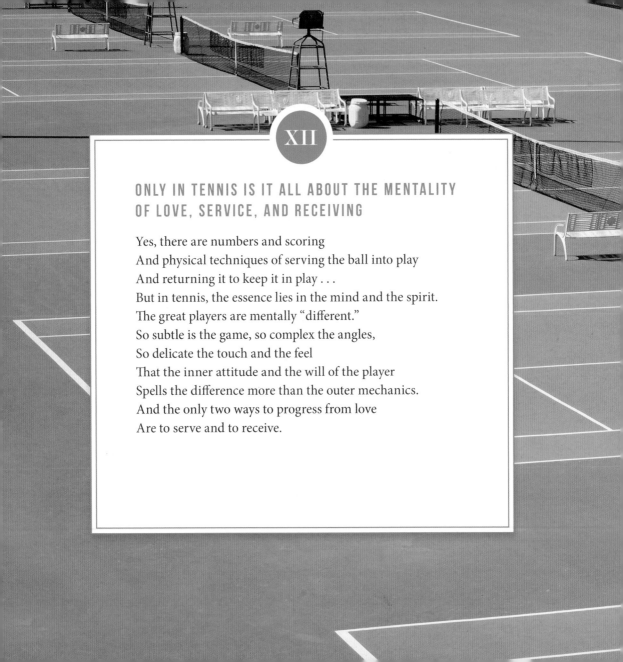

XII

ONLY IN TENNIS IS IT ALL ABOUT THE MENTALITY OF LOVE, SERVICE, AND RECEIVING

Yes, there are numbers and scoring
And physical techniques of serving the ball into play
And returning it to keep it in play . . .
But in tennis, the essence lies in the mind and the spirit.
The great players are mentally "different."
So subtle is the game, so complex the angles,
So delicate the touch and the feel
That the inner attitude and the will of the player
Spells the difference more than the outer mechanics.
And the only two ways to progress from love
Are to serve and to receive.

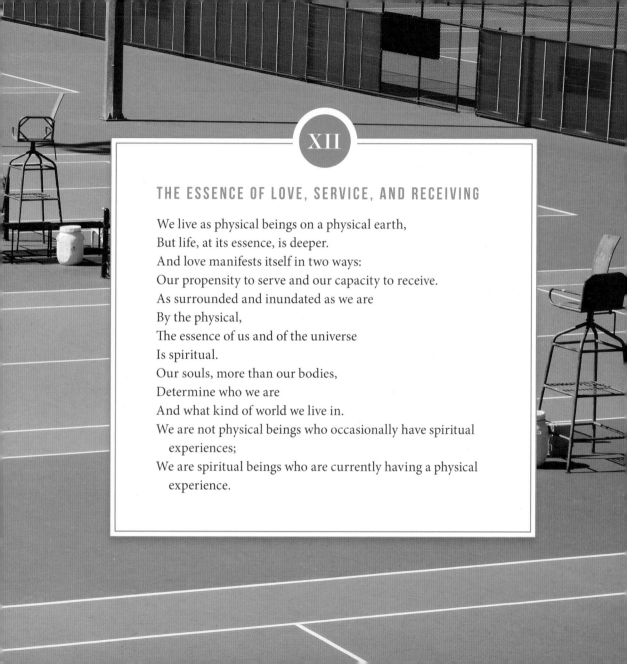

XII

THE ESSENCE OF LOVE, SERVICE, AND RECEIVING

We live as physical beings on a physical earth,
But life, at its essence, is deeper.
And love manifests itself in two ways:
Our propensity to serve and our capacity to receive.
As surrounded and inundated as we are
By the physical,
The essence of us and of the universe
Is spiritual.
Our souls, more than our bodies,
Determine who we are
And what kind of world we live in.
We are not physical beings who occasionally have spiritual
    experiences;
We are spiritual beings who are currently having a physical
    experience.

SINGLES

LONG-RANGE PARADIGMS

IN TENNIS

He'd been my nemesis for a year—simply a better, more experienced player.

We were playing every Monday evening, and for me, it was causing each week to begin with discouragement. The losing streak was making me go for too much and try too hard to put something extra on every shot.

Then one Monday, feeling relaxed after a great day at work, I shifted my perspective a bit. What was the big deal? Why was I putting so much pressure on myself? Our matches were close enough to be enjoyable. Why not just hit my best on every point and quit fearing another loss? I settled in and got rid of the jumpiness and the extra tension and the self-criticism. I saw the longer perspective. *If I lose this point, I'll win the next one; if I lose this game, I'll win the next one. If I lose the match, I'll get him next week. If I lose all year, I'll beat him next year.*

As I relaxed, I got steadily steadier, and my steadiness began to unnerve him.

I realized that I had been transferring the momentary to the eternal. *I'll never beat this guy. I'll always lose the big points.* I saw that it could work the other way instead—long-range belief stabilizing short-term perspective. *I'm in tennis for the long haul, so I should relax, enjoy, and see what I can learn today.*

I had been confusing the end with the means, approaching each match as though it were an end in itself rather than as the means to the real end of having fun, staying in shape, and gradually getting better.

IN LIFE

I t is a common and limiting mistake to confuse means and ends. And the way to overcome the tendency is to get in the good habit of asking why. *Why am I working so hard?* If the answer is to provide a better life for your family, be sure that you are not prioritizing your job over your marriage and your children. If you are, if you see work or financial successes as ends in themselves, you may one day regret confusing the means of money achievement with the end of the growth and happiness of your family.

And remembering the longer-range perspective of the true end of relationships and family can relax us and lift us a little above the stress and competition of the means of work and achievements. And in this correct perspective, we may come to understand the peaceful facts that . . .

- things take time, especially worthwhile things.
- life's setbacks and disappointments fade over time.
- good and gratitude and growth magnify over time.
- all things come to those who wait and who work and who watch.
- while instant gratification is lovely, we shouldn't expect it very often.
- the best measurement of our selves is how much we love.
- the most important work we will ever do will be within the walls of our home.[1]
- no other success can compensate for failure in the family.[2]
- relationships are the end; accomplishments and achievements are the means.

*Remembering
the longer-range
perspective of the true
end of relationships
and family can relax
us and lift us.*

THE ART OF
RECEIVING

IN TENNIS

"Hate the ball; hit it like you despise it," said my college coach. "Especially on your service return, your hatred and anger will give you extra power. That ball has infringed on your space. You own your side of the court. Get that ball out of there."

The concept didn't appeal much, but I tried it. There may indeed have been extra power, but I didn't like it—or its erratic results. One day, I decided to try the opposite: to love the ball, to be grateful for it, thankful for the opportunities and challenges it presented me with, and appreciative of its speed and the spin that I could make work for me.

I thought about how glad I was to be there, how happy I was to receive as my opponent served. "Return of service" took on a whole new meaning.

Receiving isn't so bad; too many players think of it as resisting or retaliating or retrieving. Remember, it's receiving! Take what you're given. Be complimented when it's good or when it's hard. Don't wish for the soft, the easy, the double fault.

Be the partaker, the beneficiary, the consumer, the receiver of all the variety that the game of tennis offers you. Be grateful for the hard first serves because they challenge you and make you better. Be grateful for the soft second-serve blessings because they give you new opportunities to hit winners.

IN LIFE

So much time is wasted and joy forfeited by wanting and wishing for what we don't have and taking for granted what we do have. Thinking we deserve it, we earned it, we own it, or we are entitled to it robs us of gratitude.

Instead, consider the lilies; consider the abundance. See the glass as half full, and understand that you didn't make the water nor can you walk on it.

There is joy and release in thankfulness and in humility. Take the gratitude rather than the credit—it's lighter and usually more accurate.

Love what comes at you, understanding that it's a part of the untidy, unending, unpredictable diversity that is part of this ultimate reality show called mortality.

To mix a metaphor, no matter how good the quarterback is, there has to be a good receiver, and good receivers are always positioning themselves to better receive the gifts.

Be grateful for life's challenges because they test you and make you better. Be grateful for life's blessings because they give you new opportunities for gratitude.

Consider the
lilies; consider the
abundance.

CONFIDENCE AND INTIMIDATION

IN TENNIS

Years ago, while I lived and worked in Washington, DC, I had a friend who was on the staff of the president. One day, he invited me to come over and play tennis at the White House.

The presidential court is secluded behind trees at the back of the grounds. The landscaping and magnificent old trees make it a truly beautiful place. Two cabinet members were just finishing a match. I was so impressed (and intimidated) that when we got on the court, I could barely hit the ball during the first set. I knew I was a better player than my friend, but I lost the set 6–2. As the second set started, I remembered the basketball movie *Hoosiers*, in which the small-town team comes into the huge state arena to play the big-city team for the state championship. The coach brings the wide-eyed farm boys in, pulls out a tape measure, and shows them that the baskets are ten feet and the free throw line is fifteen feet back—just like the court at home. I began to think about the regulation court rather than about the White House setting and managed to get my game back and win the next two sets.

When a place or a tournament or an opponent intimidates you in some way, remind yourself that nothing essential has changed. You are still you. It still takes just four points to win a game. The court is still seventy-eight feet long. Your racket is still the same one you won with the other day. Shut out the irrelevant.

IN LIFE

The problem with intimidation or a drop in confidence is that it freezes you, wilts you, pulls you away from your natural ability and energy, and creates mental blocks. So break it down, analyze it, and dismiss it.

I had a contrasting White House experience a few years after the tennis incident. This time, I was (unintentionally) the intimidator rather than the intimidatee. I'd received a presidential appointment to direct a White House conference and was given a wonderful, huge office in an old, classic brownstone building on Jackson Place, just across Pennsylvania Avenue. The office, thirty feet wide, had bay windows at both ends; out of one I could see the White House and out of the other the garden of Blair House where foreign heads of state stayed. An enormous cut crystal chandelier hung from the fifteen-foot ceiling. Guests and appointments would walk into my office and be so awed that they would forget their facts, sometimes even forgetting what they came for. I learned that I had to do something to relax them—take their coat, put my feet up, or tell them the office intimidated me, too.

Watching intimidation makes it easier to understand than feeling it. It's a false, silly emotion. People are people. Places are places. And neither should have the power to diminish what or how we think of ourselves. Remember that any two people always have more in common than in difference. Whatever "important" person you're thinking of puts on his or her pants the same way you do—one leg at a time—and has plenty of self-doubts of his or her own.

Bottom line: "a realization of the universal lack of self-confidence strengthens one's own."[3]

Remember that any two people always have more in common than in difference.

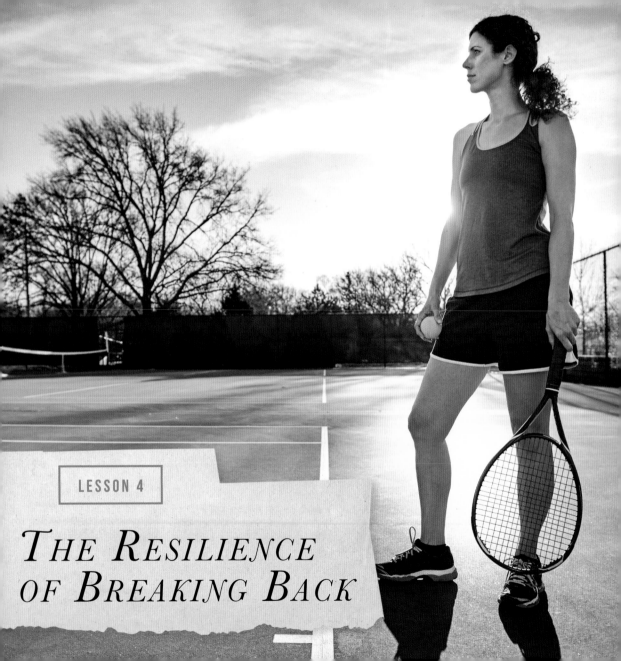

THE RESILIENCE OF BREAKING BACK

IN TENNIS

For years, I lived in Salt Lake City and watched John Stockton, the gutsy little point guard for the Utah Jazz, who holds two NBA career records that will never be broken—for assists and for steals—and who was the perfect example of bouncing back. If he made a turnover or missed a shot or if his man got by his defense, you could almost count on him making a steal or an assist or some kind of big play the next time down the court.

The tennis equivalent is breaking back. When you lose your service, your best chance to break back is in the very next game. Your opponent has expended a lot of effort for his break and may let up a bit or be mentally overconfident. If he holds, he'll get stronger. But if you break back now, everything returns to parity and you even gain mental advantages by having made his lead so short lived.

Technically, a person who always breaks back can never lose two sets in a row. If your opponent served first, he could win the first set (if you both held until 5–4 and then he got the first break for 6–4). But your break back would put you up 1–0 in the second set. He could not win the match so long as you broke back any time you were broken.

Breaking back is a mindset. It is a resiliency and toughmindedness that allows a player to dig down and make a habit of getting games back.

Evonne Goolagong said, "A break is not a break until you hold." So you deny your opponent a break when you break back. One player preferred to call it a "bend," which became a break only if he failed to return the favor the next game.

IN LIFE

There are so many variations of being broken in life: big ones like a business failure or a devastating divorce, medium ones like being passed over for a promotion or not getting into your first-choice graduate school, and small ones like missing a flight or having an argument with your spouse or your significant other.

One of the true measures of a person is how he responds. Does the break cause discouragement and despondency and doubts, thus feeding on itself and leading to further failure? Or does it create determination and dig-in dedication that brings him back even stronger?

The best timing for a break back is *fast*. If you wallow in something, it compounds itself. While you're down on the diving board, it has the spring to catapult you up beyond where you started. Breaks can have net gain. If a rung breaks on your ladder and you drop down, you climb again by stepping over the broken rung and up to the next highest step.

By learning from mistakes, not repeating them, and stepping up over them, we end up ahead. Reparation or repentance may be a part of it. Where you've made mistakes, correct them, apologize where necessary, make amends, receive forgiveness, and put things right. Break back and move forward.

The best timing for a break back is fast.

PRAISE VERSUS CRITICISM

IN TENNIS

As I write this chapter, I'm in the process of teaching my youngest child—a daughter, ten years old—to play tennis. Some would say ten is too late, and others would say you're crazy to try to teach your own child.

But I feel much less pressure with Charity than I did with some of her older siblings. She's more of a musician (a flutist) and dancer right now. It's not important to her to be competitive at tennis. She wants to play for fun. As a result—and this is the point—I've never felt any need to criticize her, to point out the flaws in her strokes, to break down every part of her game and analyze it and correct it. Instead, I just show her things and praise her every attempt. When she misses, I just praise the *try*. When I watch her and notice three things wrong and one thing right, I talk just about the one positive thing. This isn't something I've done consciously . . . it's just that she's my last child and I enjoy her so much. My relationship with her and the self-esteem I want her to have are more important to me than how good she gets at tennis.

Now here's the thing: she loves it and she is getting better fast. She asks me for lessons because she enjoys them. There's none of the tension I felt with some of my other kids as I pressed them.

Tennis is a game of confidence and self-esteem. Most players, even learners, know pretty much what they're doing right and what they're doing wrong. They need a little tip or suggestion here and there, but they don't need criticism or self-consciousness-creating pressure, either from others or from themselves.

IN LIFE

In all our important relationships (with spouses, with children, with ourselves), praise is more helpful and more effective (as well as more pleasant) than criticism.

Family members generally know their faults and are likely to feel resentful when they are continually reminded of them, especially by someone they look up to and are trying to please.

Everyone—and children particularly—tend to live up to their reputation. If our constant criticism, correction, and castigation give them a perceived reputation of being slow, inept, unruly, sloppy, or rebellious, chances are that they will live up to it.

On the other hand, if our praise gives them a perceived reputation of being brave, of being good, or of being sensitive, chances are that they will live up to it.

We should try harder to make our children *happy* and less hard to make them *good*. And we will find that what makes them happy will ultimately make them good.

Everyone—and children particularly—tend to live up to their reputation.

RIGHT MAKES MIGHT

IN TENNIS

One of the great tennis stories of integrity and reputation comes out of a match between Stan Smith and Arthur Ashe. Smith scrambled in for a drop shot, and the chair umpire couldn't tell if he got it before it bounced. Smith nodded, saying he did, and the umpire looked across to Ashe. Arthur said simply, "If Stan says he got it, he got it."

There is power in integrity and weakness in its lack. Never call a questionable ball out. In fact, correct yourself if your instinct yells "out" but your eyes don't confirm it. Do it for two reasons: (1) it's the right thing to do and (2) it makes you stronger, and you will win the next point 75 percent of the time. There are takers and there are givers when it comes to line calls, and both reputations follow you quietly around.

And right not only makes might but it also makes friends. We love opponents who give the benefit of the doubt, who call our close ones "in," and we dislike playing those who call every close ball we hit "out."

Many things in a tennis match are beyond our control, but we can always control how honestly we play it.

IN LIFE

Rationalizing, stretching, exaggerating, hedging . . . they are all bad ideas, and they can all turn into bad habits. And they are not worth it. Compare what you gain with what you lose—a thimbleful of advantage, a bucketful of angst. Eye-meeting honesty is the real advantage: disarming, direct, strength-giving, simplifying. What you see is what you get.

There are a lot of things in life over which we have no control. But the one thing we can always control is our response to *things*. It is always within our power to choose whether to get angry or remain calm, whether to judge someone or give him the benefit of the doubt, whether to be truthful or deceptive.

One meaning for the mathematical term "congruence" is a total consistency between what we say and what we know, between how we act and who we are. Those who are fully congruent gain a kind of strength and trust that those who design their truth to suit their needs and their advantage can never find.

*Eye-meeting
honesty is the
real advantage:
disarming, direct,
strength-giving,
simplifying.*

LESSON 7

DON'T MISS SHORT (AVOID THE NET)

IN TENNIS

A tennis coach friend of mine says the key thing he tries to teach beginners is to think of overcoming obstacles one at a time. The first obstacle is the net, so the first thing to concentrate on is getting the ball over the net. "Don't miss short" or "If you're going to miss, miss long." Then the second obstacle is the confining length of the court, but that doesn't even come into play until the ball goes over the net. Once balls are going over the net, then start worrying about keeping them in the court.

Except for carefully disguised drop shots, short balls are weak. They put you on the defensive. Hit long and worry later about "too long." Go for it. Better to miss the baseline than to dump the ball into the net. Better to just miss a deep winner than to let the net rob you of any chance or to give your opponent an easy, shallow ball.

Ironically, the great tennis fear of unforced errors can only be eased by actually *making* errors. Try it and miss. Try it again. Learn from every miss. Learn from every loss. And don't come back more cautious; come back bigger. The bigger the point, the bigger the shot you hit. Go big! Recognize that you have a greater chance of missing when you take something off than when you hit out.

'Tis better to have hit all out and missed than to have never hit out at all.

IN LIFE

In our family, we'd been trying to get the kids to memorize special sayings. (We felt the memorizing itself was good mental discipline, and we hoped the quotes we'd chosen would be like little implants that would be in there with them when they needed something.) One week, we all memorized the Shakespeare phrase "Our doubts are traitors and make us lose the good we oft might win by failing to attempt." Eli, who was seven at the time and one of our best memorizers, seemed to particularly like the quote.

Two years later when the NBA had its all-star game in our city, we were at a pre-event where kids could participate in various basketball contests.

Eli's brothers were in the slam-dunk contest, and there was a lower-basket nine-to-ten-year-old division, but the arena full of people was intimidating to Eli, and I couldn't get him to enter. I focused on the other boys and forgot about Eli until suddenly I heard his name announced. He had gone down and entered. After three rounds of competition, Eli ended up as the winner of his division.

Afterward, he explained, "I was just sitting there, and suddenly I thought, 'My doubts are traitors,' so I decided to go down and go for it!"

A moment later, he said, "Even if I hadn't won, I'd be glad I tried it." Jumping out of our comfort zone can be the difference between boredom and exhilaration.

We all need to decide to "go on down and go for it." Life is not a dress rehearsal. *Involvement* and *trying* and *experiencing* and *participating* are what make up real life.

Life is not a dress rehearsal.

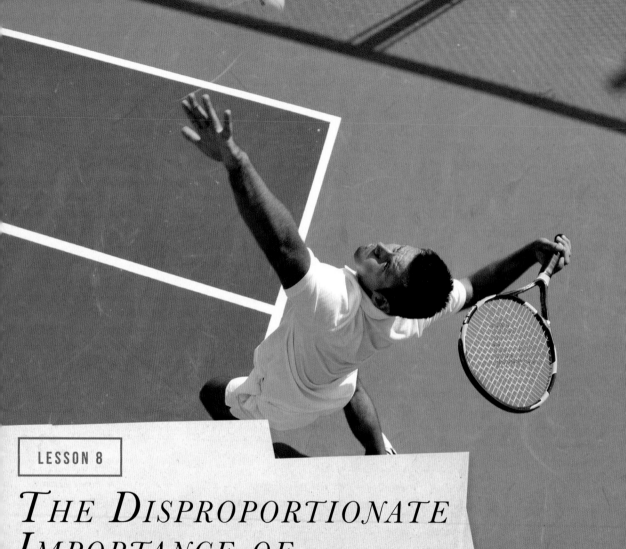

THE DISPROPORTIONATE IMPORTANCE OF BEGINNINGS AND ENDS

IN TENNIS

Starting strong is the key to so many matches. Getting that first hold or two and going all out for an early break not only shakes your opponent but also lifts your game and infuses it with confidence. It becomes the basis for belief. If you come out purposeful and energized and committed, even your misses send a message and set the tone.

Just as the first games can be the most important of the match, the first point can be the most important of a game. Getting ahead, even by a point, and then feeling strong and building on that little success can start momentum. Great players rarely "feel their way" into a match. They come out strong. They execute early and get a lead, and then they ride that confidence throughout the match.

The only thing more important than how you start is how you close. Those who watched him and particularly those who played against him said that what separated Rod Laver from everyone else in his era was that he always raised his level when he saw the finish line. His last, close-out games were always his best.

It's not that the middle part of a match is unimportant. It's just that with a strong start and a strong finish, the middle most often takes care of itself.

IN LIFE

Don't let a new day just come upon you.

Start it proactively in whatever is your way: a prayer, a run, a written plan.

Or start it by thinking hard and listing three choose-to-dos before you get to the list of have-to dos.

One way is to get up each day and accomplish one or two little things right away—maybe make one phone call or write one little memo; maybe clean up the kitchen or mow the front lawn; do something early, before breakfast, something to build on for the rest of the day—a little success to set a pattern for the day, a little fulfillment, a minor satisfaction as an appetizer. It's a good feeling and it sets the tone for the day to just keep getting better and better.

End the day equally strong—a journal entry, a text to a loved one, a quick list of the day's blessings, something that matters, something that impacts a priority. Close it out strong and thoughtfully and then sleep with good dreams.

Starting strong can apply to *weeks* as well as days—a great habit is to devote a part of each Sunday to *planning* the week ahead. And it can apply to months—time spent the first day of a month calendaring and projecting and goal-setting. And it can apply to years—making New Year's resolutions that are strong and practical and clear.

Beginnings and *ends* of any kind are inherently important—the beginning of a relationship, of a conversation, of a meeting, of a speech, or of a journey. Make the effort and the mental commitment to start and finish strong.

*Don't let a new day
just come upon you.*

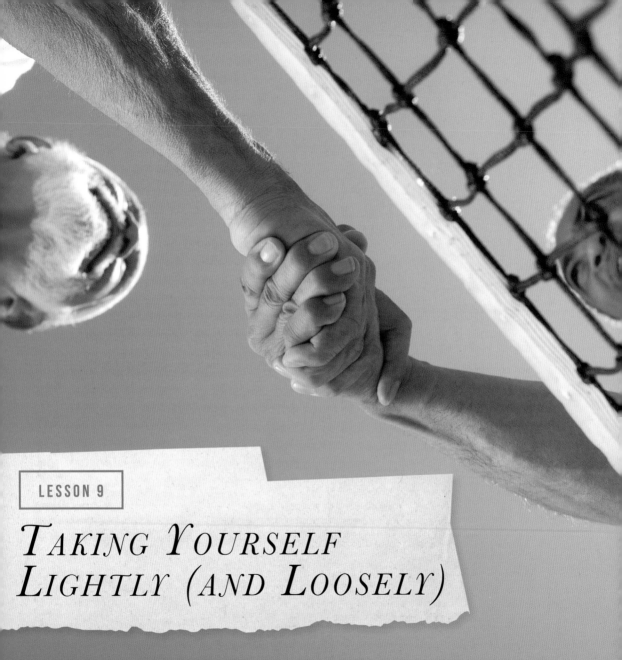

TAKING YOURSELF LIGHTLY (AND LOOSELY)

IN TENNIS

That familiar (but unwelcome) tightness and lack of timing seems to come more when we play a new opponent. Everything's uncertain. You don't know him or his game, and he doesn't know you. One way to ease tension—to loosen up and start feeling more relaxed about yourself—is simply to *talk*. Talk to your opponent after you walk on the court, during warm-up, or when you come to the net to spin for serve.

Find out who he is, where he lives, what he does. Notice things about him—things that are vulnerable, things that make him enjoyable to play, his weaknesses and strengths, things that make him human and non-intimidating. By focusing your interest and attention on your opponent, you take your mind off yourself and lose the self-consciousness that robs your natural timing and flow.

And take yourself lightly. We sometimes play tennis as though it were an obligation, a responsibility, as though the destiny of the world hung on the outcome, or as though our whole persona and self-image were somehow tied up in how we hit our shots or how many games we won.

The fact is that tennis is a *game* . . . and a game should be *played*. A game is for fun. The point of the game is enjoyment and relaxation. It is a game that should be played with lightness, with good humor, with abandon.

As a player learns to take himself more *lightly* on the court, the term takes on triple levels of related meaning—he becomes *lighter* on his feet, quicker; his mind feels more *enlightened*, aware and clear about what to do; and he sees and feels the *lighter* side of the game, the humor and the fun of just being out there swatting that little fuzzy yellow ball.

IN LIFE

Tension in new relationships, new situations, and unexpected or unplanned or unfamiliar circumstances can seem to grow on us if we don't do something to cut through it.

I remember my first day as a student at the Harvard Business School. I was intimidated in that classroom full of one hundred of the "best and brightest." But someone had advised me to raise my hand and participate at the very first opportunity, told me that the longer I waited, the harder it would get. So I did. What I said wasn't very consequential, but the next participation was a little easier, and I loosened up fairly quickly—particularly as I noticed others who looked more uptight than I was.

Both tennis and life are games, and it's okay to think of them this way. Life can be a very complex game with very large consequences, but most of it, on the day to day, is fairly routine and not terribly consequential.

"Don't sweat the small stuff . . . and it's all small stuff."[4] Or as G. K. Chesterton put it: "Angels can fly because they can take themselves lightly."[5]

We can *learn* how to take ourselves lightly, and it is a wonderful skill to have.

"Lightly" has a triple meaning in life as well. It means *humor*, seeing the ironies, the light moments, being able to laugh at ourselves. It means *weightlessness* or less weight, being up, feeling less heavy or burdened down. And it means *inspired*, illuminated, and insightful. The three meanings (the three great qualities) go together and feed off each other.

We can learn how to take ourselves lightly, and it is a wonderful skill to have.

LESSON 10

KEEP MOVING FORWARD

IN TENNIS

"Keep moving forward. Don't hit off of your back foot. Lean in. Don't guide it." These were like mantras to a coach I liked. And he was right. Winning doesn't happen when you are backing up. When you are moving forward, you are on the offense, your weight is flowing into the shot, and your balls are deeper and heavier.

Be proactive at every opportunity, no matter how early or how late it is in the match.

This lesson applies to all sports. Inevitably, when a team goes conservative or stalls too early, players lose momentum, lose timing, and lose point margin to the more aggressive team who is attempting a comeback.

But it applies most of all to tennis, where there isn't a clock; you can never win by simply keeping the points you already have and waiting for the game to end. The game doesn't end until you win or lose the final point. Stalling is pointless. Yet so often, a player with a lead plays like he just wants to preserve what he has, like he wants the match to end right where it is. He forgets that he came to play, that the points in the future are like the points in the past, that the kind of play that got him ahead will keep him ahead, and that slowing up or "preserving" will only take the flow and timing out of his game and give his opponent opportunities to rally.

Instead, turn it up! Build on your lead and on your momentum. Use the *freedom* that a lead gives you to take more risks, to go for harder shots. Just as a wealthy person has the freedom to travel more widely, try more things, and invest where there are higher rewards, so a player with a lead has freedom to step up and move forward to the next level.

IN LIFE

Life's equivalent to stalling or protecting your lead is resting on your laurels. Anytime you say (or think), "I've arrived," "I've just got to protect what I've got," or "This is the level where I want to stay," you're in trouble.

Life isn't static. There is always movement—either forward or back. And life isn't about arriving; it is a journey that is not over until it's over. (Many people of faith believe it is a journey that never ends.)

Just as in tennis, there is no set clock, no prescribed time limit; in life, the winning score or required number of points is not even known. So if we're in a preserving mode, stalling, trying to just stay on the rung we're on, resting on our laurels, what is the point? Life is still happening, and we're missing it. Are we like bears or squirrels that work hard accumulating fat or nuts so they can hibernate or stay in their tree?

Perhaps someone who was injured or impaired, who could not progress or experience much, or someone with a known, short time to live might be justified in "stalling." Yet, ironically, people like this—with six months to live—usually live to the fullest, experiencing and progressing at an accelerated rate in their remaining time.

One of the fastest-growing Christian religions in the world states that mankind's goal is "eternal progression"—no time clock, no final score, no end of game, but a continual, joyful progression from level to level, using what we have to help others and to go beyond where we have been.

In life, don't stall too soon . . . and it's always too soon. Instead, move forward.

Life isn't static. There is always movement—either forward or back.

TRANSFORM ANGER

IN TENNIS

Just thinking of *anger* and *tennis* brings stereotypical images to mind: a player yelling at an umpire, throwing his racket, smacking a ball over the fence. The delicacy and finesse and touch of the game create frustration in their absence.

The most common form of tennis anger is anger at self—negative self-talk—and nothing destroys your game faster.

Yet anger is by definition an energizing emotion. Are the best players those who never feel it—the cool, icy, mechanical players who look and act the same after hitting an unforced error as after hitting a winner? Or have good players just learned to channel their emotions into the power of their shots?

The emotionless approach won't work for most of us. Telling yourself not to feel anger is probably just going to make you mad! Use a little psychology on yourself; *welcome* the anger but transform it into concentration and power. See frustration and annoyance as tools that can be channeled into your feet and your arm and add strength to the next shot.

IN LIFE

Generally speaking, there are two broad types of anger or frustration (we're not talking about violent, psychopathic anger here, just the normal, day-to-day annoyances and irritations). One is the frustration you can do nothing about: sitting in traffic congestion, dealing with some slow-moving bureaucracy, anything over which you have no control. The other is the type of frustration we can control: anger with our own procrastination or forgetfulness or timidity or lack of self-control, forgetting an appointment, breaking our diet, missing an opportunity.

We need to learn to consciously separate the two because they have different solutions. With one, we need to learn to *release*; with the other, we need to learn to *transform*.

Anger and frustration are cumulative and collective. They can kind of pool up inside us, getting deeper and deeper. So we need to get our drainage set, to have ways to channel the feelings out as they come in so they never begin to collect. With the frustrations you can't do anything about, the key word is *release*—never dam them up but concentrate on just letting them flow through you and out of you.

With self-frustration, transform it like a high-pressure fire hose—focus it on a change you want to make and use its pressure and power to make something better.

With the frustrations you can't do anything about, the key word is release—never dam them up but concentrate on just letting them flow through you and out of you.

GET A LITTLE COACHING NOW AND THEN

IN TENNIS

I was playing on the clay courts in New York's Central Park, and Nick Bollettieri happened to be giving a lesson on the next court. We chatted briefly, and he gave me a small tip—a little thing he had observed in my game. I've never forgotten it.

There are three broad kinds of improvement in tennis: (1) the attitudinal and mental improvements this book will bring you to; (2) the conditioning, learning, and muscle-memory improvements that practice and playing bring; and (3) a new technique or tip that might come from your own observation but is more likely to come from someone else who is more objective and knows more about certain aspects of the game than you do.

Pro tennis players have coaches—coaches who watch them objectively and try to add something to the mix. Sometimes one little thing—a slightly altered grip, a shorter backswing on one type of shot, a little different footwork on a backhand volley—can make a big difference, can change our confidence level, and can help us see or understand something we were missing.

Perhaps most importantly, a little coaching or an occasional lesson can get us away from the status quo, remove us from a rut, help us remember that the goal is to get better.

It's important to keep in mind that coaches or teachers work for us. Don't give them too much control over your game. Don't get too reliant on them. Don't begin to think of yourself as trying to please them or become like them. Let them help you decide what your game needs, and let them help you develop what you decide you want. But remember that they're your goals and that it's your game—and that there is a lot your coach doesn't know.

IN LIFE

No matter how hard you work, no matter how good your education or training is, no matter how much you know, there are people who know things (even about your life, your job, your family) that you don't, people who have discovered things you haven't and who can see you more objectively than you can see yourself.

We all need a little coaching now and then. Even if lots of what we are taught are things we already know, it's reminding us that we need to progress, that life isn't about staying where we are. Often, just one new perspective or a glimpse into a different paradigm or a little tip or new approach can make a truly significant difference.

I remember going to a seminar conducted by my good friend Stephen Covey (who, by the way, was a deceptively good tennis player). The seminar was on his *7 Habits of Highly Effective People*, but he referenced family and parenting a lot. I think of myself as something of a parenting expert, having written some books on the subject and having raised several pretty great kids, but I went home with pages of notes, with some new ideas, and with renewed commitment. I still remember the concept of "an emotional bank account" that you deposit into every time you spend meaningful, loving time with a child, an account you can draw on in times of trouble or stress.

Seminars, analysts, teachers, consultants, advisors, self-help books—whatever your choice or whatever your need is—get a little coaching. But not too much! And don't give up control. Be a positive critic of all advice and accept only what rings true to your heart.

Be a positive critic of all advice and accept only what rings true to your heart.

Outlast Your Opponents (Live Long)

IN TENNIS

I t is a great feeling to be on the court starting a third set and to look over at your opponent and know you've got more left than he does—to realize that you're in better shape and that you are going to outlast him and win the match.

There are two kinds of strength and joy in having trained hard and taken care of yourself. One is simply feeling good. The other is the anticipation of good shots yet to come—shots you wouldn't have had the opportunity to hit if you hadn't hung in until now, if you hadn't been in good enough shape to grind it out. For most of us who play, tennis is a way of getting and staying in shape as well as a reason for wanting to be healthy and in condition.

When you take care of your body, you're able to get to things you otherwise couldn't. You're able to get to a ball that would have gone past you; you're able to get to opponents who would otherwise get to you. And you're able to get to third sets and to tiebreakers that otherwise would have never happened.

In the longer term, "outlasting your opponents" has a whole other dimension. Being in condition and taking care of yourself is what allows you to keep playing the game and, as the years go by, to enjoy getting a little older and a little smarter. Persistence is strength. Maybe you are the tenth best player in your club in the 60s division, but by the 65s, you might be number five simply because five of those ahead of you have quit playing singles. By the 70s, maybe you are number three, by the 75s, number two, and maybe in the 80s, you are, finally, number one.

IN LIFE

In a world moving and changing as fast as ours, those who experience and accomplish the most, who get the furthest and reach closest to their full potential, may simply be those who live the longest.

I desperately want to live into the middle part of the twenty-first century. I want to see what the world is like by then, what has been discovered, what is possible, what I can accomplish and experience by then, who and what and where my children and grandchildren and great-grandchildren will be by then. And since I was born in the middle part of the twentieth century, my goal won't be easy.

I've got a great friend for a doctor with whom I've shared this longevity goal. He runs tests on everything and advises me. I work at staying in shape, on how I eat, on my attitudes, on my blood pressure, on my cholesterol, and on my body fat. It's not an obsession, and it's not vanity. It's curiosity and adventure and an intense desire to be around for a long time.

As in tennis, there are two advantages: one is just that I feel good, and the other is that sense of *anticipation mixed with patience*. I'm excited to do and see so much, but I don't have to do it all at once or right now. I can take the longer view, be more selective, and let things come to me.

Of course, there are no guarantees. As in tennis, you may meet an opponent who knocks you out quickly no matter how hard you've worked at being in condition. But taking care of yourself is still a no-brainer decision because you'll enjoy more every day you do have left and care better for those you love during whatever time frame you have with them.

Take the longer view, be more selective, and let things come.

THE JOY OF REJOICING (THERE ARE ALWAYS TWO OBJECTIVES)

IN TENNIS

How many times have you seen it: A player hits a couple of bad shots on crucial points or misses an easy overhead and can't seem to get over it. He yells at himself (something nasty or sarcastic) and then mopes around the court, missing the shots he was hitting a few minutes ago and carping to himself about the key shot he missed or about how he can't play the big points. Sometimes the funk lasts for several games, sometimes for the rest of the match.

Too often, when the same player smacks a clean winner, he'll take it for granted instead of feeding off of it. He may say, "It's about time" or "Well, what do you know, one went in," almost implying that he probably won't do it again.

Great players learn to do just the opposite. When they miss a shot, they shake it off quickly, thinking of it as a fluke, not dwelling on it even for a moment, digging in with extra determination for the next point. And when they hit a screamer down the line or an ace or a clean volley winner, they rejoice with a pump of the fist or a hop of self-confidence or just a mental "congratulations" that essentially says, "That was fun. I'm going to remember the feel of that. I want a lot more of those."

Cultivate a feeling of joy and well-being while you play. Look up at the mountains or the trees or whatever beauty surrounds the court. Appreciate the sun or the indoor lights or the clean white lines. Think how happy you are just to be there, to be playing. Be as glad about not being injured as you would be sad if you were. Putting your mind on joy or beauty will take your mind off of yourself, which is what all good players try to do. Rejoice more, and your game will soon give you more to rejoice about.

Remember that in tennis, there are always two goals. One is to win, and the other is to enjoy. Don't let your focus on the first one rob you of the second one.

IN LIFE

Most people are actually better at sorrow than they are at joy. Maybe it's an easier emotion. When something goes wrong or doesn't work out, we're good at regretting it, resenting it, and feeling bad about it for a long time. We play it through again and again in our minds, wishing we'd done something differently and thinking "What if" or "If only."

But when something good happens—maybe even the "If only" or "What if" we were wishing for—we're momentarily happy about it, and then we begin taking it for granted, moving on mentally to our next wish.

Why do we so often let good moments pass and die and keep the negative or sad ones alive for so long? We should strive to flip it. Deal with the disappointments or failures—whatever they require—but move on quickly, putting them behind you literally and mentally. Think of it as an exception, out of the ordinary, ended right now, unlikely to repeat.

What if we could feel the same intensity and "length" in our rejoicing as we do in our sadness or regret?

When there is a success or even a spontaneous moment of joy, seize it, savor it, be *grateful* for it, feel it all over. Be humble about it, but be pleased. It's okay to feel joy. Indeed, it's why we are here! Rejoice in it, pass it on to others, record it in a journal, and be looking (and expecting) to repeat it or find something equally good. Cultivate joy by noticing any little instance of anything that brings it. Grab it as it goes by and hang on.

Whatever objective you are working on, remember that there is another, overlying goal—to enjoy the journey.

When there is a success or even a spontaneous moment of joy, seize it, savor it, be grateful for it, feel it all over.

THE CONSTANT
QUEST FOR WINNERS

IN TENNIS

Have you ever had a little injury that slows you down and forces you to try to shorten the points? You go for early winners and what you learn is that you have more offense—more power, more angles, more *winners*—in your game than you had realized.

Like so many tennis terms, "winners" are perfectly named. You hit one and you *win* the point. It's over. It's money in the bank.

And winners are the goal—the ongoing, ever-present goal—of every point. As obvious as that sounds, players tend to forget it. They play as though the goal is "keeping the ball in play" or "getting the ball back" or "not missing." These may be the goals on certain shots or in certain situations when one is forced to the defense, but if we get too used to these goals, we forget about *winners*—we forget the glory and satisfaction of them and lose our familiarity with them and our passion for them.

Have you ever been down a couple of breaks and figured the first set was gone—so you loosen up and start going for more winners, figuring you'll expend less energy that way and maybe get your strokes grooved for the second set? And then, just when you'd stopped thinking about winning that set, you start winning. Your shots have more zip, you're quicker and easier to the ball, your timing is better, and you're instinctively making the right shot selection.

What's happened? You started thinking less and going for winners. Ponder this a little and understand that caution and hesitation and worry about the score harms your tennis—then practice going for winners and taking risks until it feels natural and habitual.

IN LIFE

In life, as well as in tennis, one must understand each of his individual capacities and know just when to use them based on a total awareness of exactly where he is and where his opposition is.

The magic of staying focused on the goal and on seeing and using every opening or opportunity to get to the goal works similarly for a winner in tennis, for checkmate in chess, or for reaching an objective in life.

We have to remember that getting up and having breakfast and going to work and putting in our time may be the routine necessity of life, and it may be noble and responsible, but it is not the goal any more than conditioning or hitting nice, consistent ground strokes is the goal of tennis.

The self-discipline and putting in the hours and the effort is good but not as an end in itself. It is good (like staying in the point in tennis) because it sets you up to see and reach the real objective (like seeing and hitting the real winner).

Sometimes—like being behind in the first set—a little setback in life is what causes us to go for it a little stronger and a little more consciously toward our objectives, to spend a little less time going through the motions, and to draw on our full power and best "angles" to get it done.

How do we keep doing it that way? Once again, the answer is in our attitude. When we consciously adopt the attitude of going for winners and taking calculated risks, when this attitude is in focus and in priority in our minds, we stay out of ruts, we seize the opportunities, and we enjoy life more.

*When we consciously adopt the attitude of going for
winners and taking calculated risks, when this attitude
is in focus and in priority in our minds, we stay out of
ruts, we seize the opportunities, and we enjoy life more.*

THE RELEVANCE OF
INTERMEDIATE GOALS

IN TENNIS

In a match, of course, the long-range goal is to win. The shorter-range goal is to win the point.

Even shorter: hit the next shot well.

But a match can be long and unpredictable and may require a lot of adjustments along the way. Hitting good shots and winning points does not actually count for anything unless you string together enough of them to get a game.

The points on the scoreboard go away after every game. It's games that count, that stay in the score, and that make up sets. It's the intermediate goals of winning games and winning a set that makes the difference. Good, strategic tennis thinking focuses on games and sets. When we concentrate on them, the longer-term match and the shorter-term point will take care of themselves. Keep your mind on the intermediate goal of winning the more "lasting" game.

Here is the way to think about that goal: it takes only four points to win a tennis game, and your opponent will almost always give you at least one of them. So just win three points. Three is a stable, triangular number. A first and a last and a middle. Thinking that way makes the game simple. Say to yourself, "Win three" and then get one. Then think, "One down, two to go" and get another. Then say, "Two down, one to go" and get it. Game over. On to the next. Do it again. Keep it simple. One, two, three.

There will be a lot of strokes in there—back-and-forth rallies. But just hit three that win—three that are winners, and the game is yours. Do that six times and you have accomplished the second intermediate goal. Then start over, get the first intermediate goal six times, and the match is over.

IN LIFE

In life, of course, the longest-range goals are to succeed, to be happy, to live well, and to care for and ensure the well-being of those you love. The shortest-range goal is to have good days and good hours and good moments. The problem is that the longest range is hard to imagine, hard to grasp, and hard to focus on all at once. And the shortest-range individual days and hours are so unpredictable and fluid that they are hard to control.

It's the weeks, the months, and the years that count—the intermediate segments of life—where adjustments can be made, where a bad day can be overcome by working hard at a couple of good ones, where an off month can be learned from and spun into a better following month.

Good strategic thinking focuses on weekly goals leading to monthly goals leading to yearly goals leading to five-year goals. It is these intermediate objectives that connect the short-range days with the long-range, well-lived life.

Plan your days, yes, but see them as the means to reach the weeks' ends. Yearn for the life you dream of, but see those life goals as the template for the weeks, months, years, and five-year blocks whose set-and-met goals will get you to that end.

It only takes three or four well-executed deeds to win a week. And you will probably just fall into at least one of them. Someone will hand you a little opportunity or a compliment or a favor. So just pick three things you want to do in a week. One for your family, one for your work, and one for yourself. Three things that really matter, that will make a difference. Three well-thought-out goals will win a week, four of those weeks will win a month, twelve of those will win a year, and five of those will win a five-year era of your life.

It's the intermediate goals that count.

It's the intermediate goals that count.

RELISH THE BIG POINTS

IN TENNIS

I was playing in a national age group tournament at the beautiful seaside La Jolla Beach and Tennis Club. It was my first year in a higher-age division, and I felt I was younger and moved better than most of those I would play. It was certainly true of my first opponent. He was a teaching pro from Las Vegas but was a little heavy and not very mobile, and I relaxed during the warm-up, thinking that with a little placement and little pace, I would breeze past him.

Game after game, I felt in control until it got to ad or deuce, and then he found something extra—and he did it every game. He turned it up on the big points. He became more intense when it mattered. I was lucky to win three or four games in the whole match.

The lesson: not all points are created equal. Telling yourself to just hit it like you do at home in practice may help relax you, but in big matches and on big points, you have to raise your game and find another level.

Most players tighten up on the big points; it's natural to fear these big points a bit. But the best players, the ones who are used to winning, relish the big points and rise to their challenge. How many times have you seen a Federer or a Djokovic seem to just coast along until a break point and then find another gear and win the game?

Try talking yourself into loving the bigs. When you have or face a break point, say, "Ahhh, this is what I live for, this is where I shine, this is where I focus, this is where I turn it up."

IN LIFE

The one silver lining of losing that first round at La Jolla was that I got home earlier to help with the details for our son Noah's wedding, which was only a week away. While flying home, I began to think about the overwhelming importance of his wedding day. I'd been telling him to relax, not to worry, that all would be well and to just be himself, that the sun would come up and go down just like any other day.

But, I realized, it's not true! It will be *unlike* any other day. The sun will rise brighter. The very air will be full of crystals. It will be a day of vast importance and extraordinary joy! I ended up writing Noah a poem of anticipation about his wedding day during the flight home. One stanza of it went like this:

> A volcano erupts, a sun burns out,
> A black hole implodes into a galaxy,
> And all are small changes
> Compared to what happens on this day.

In life, we need to recognize the big days and even the semi-big days. When we have a big event, a big opportunity, a big idea, a big change, a big anything, we need to relish it, get up for it, and anticipate it. We need to rise above our "norm" and fully appreciate it and fully live it.

Don't dread the big meeting or the key interview or the important case. This is what you've trained for; this is what you live for. This is what makes life exciting and unpredictable.

Relish the big days and the big moments, and remember them forever.

Relish the big days and the big moments, and remember them forever.

GRATITUDE AND STEWARDSHIP

IN TENNIS

Definition: **stew•ard•ship**: something you have a sacred responsibility for

I'd had one of those drawn-out winter colds, or maybe it was the flu, but I hadn't felt well enough to play tennis for nearly two weeks. When I finally got back on the court again, I didn't expect much out of myself, but I played surprisingly well and I *enjoyed* the match as much as any I'd ever played. I sat courtside for a while afterward trying to figure out why everything felt so good. In a way, it was obvious: a simple case of "absence makes the heart grow fonder"—but it was more than that. I was appreciating the gift of my body. It felt good—I could run and swing and breathe and sweat again.

The gratitude and *stewardship* I felt for my body, for my skill, for the freedom that allowed me to play—these were not things I earned or owned; they were gifts, and they not only made me happy, they made me *better*. Instead of thinking *critically* about my game or my strategy or my strokes, I was thinking *gratefully* about the joy of just being there and about what I'd been given.

There are two opposite extremes for thinking about a physical body and skill: (1) take it for granted and squander it and (2) take pride and ownership of it.

But there is a third alternative that avoids both the abdication of the first and the conceit of the second: it is the stewardship paradigm that gratefully accepts the gift of a body and a skill that allows you enjoy a sport you love. You take care of the gift and work to improve it—not out of pride but out of gratitude.

IN LIFE

We get so caught up with the erroneous notion of ownership. When we think we own things, we are always at least a little envious, jealous, or resentful (because someone owns more) or a little prideful, superior, and condescending (because someone owns less). When we think of our talents or skills as something we own, we find ourselves constantly comparing and always dissatisfied.

For a person of faith, it is apparent that ownership is an inaccuracy—God owns all and we are mere stewards. And even a more secular mind will usually conclude that ownership is an illusion—that things pass through our hands just as we pass through time, and that this world and all that is in it belongs to the universe and not to us.

If our paradigm is ownership, we tend to feel protective, guarded, preoccupied with our stuff. Then we feel the need to hoard and control everything we own. The mentality spreads over into people. We imagine that we *own* our spouse and our kids, and we become preoccupied with pride and gummed up with greed.

However, if our paradigm is one of stewardship, we are grateful for and appreciative of all we have. We're "just happy to be here," and we feel less pressure, less selfishness, and less jealousy. We recognize that each person's stewardship is unique and that what matters is how well we care for them. People become more important to us as things become less. The gratitude and appreciation that comes relaxes us and improves our performance as well as our attitude.

If our paradigm is one of stewardship, we are grateful for and appreciative of all we have.

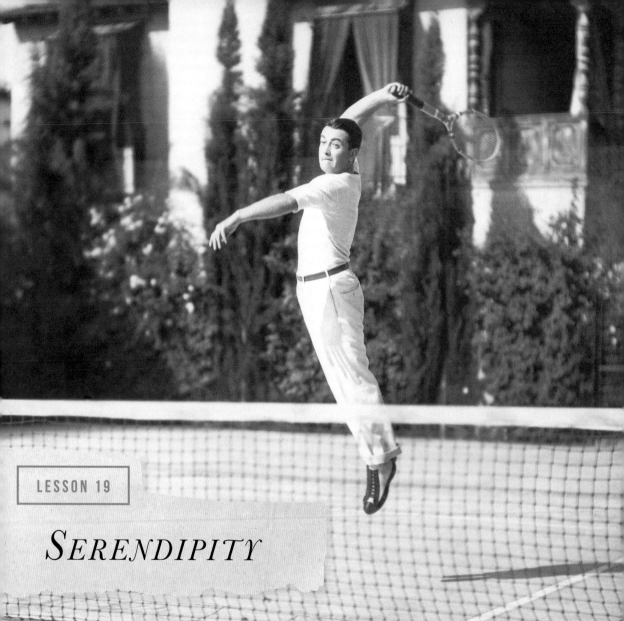

SERENDIPITY

IN TENNIS

One day after losing again to my nemesis (and his killer forehand), I asked myself what my best shot was. Surprisingly, the answer was "I don't have one."

That led to the thought that while I don't have one overpowering shot, I do have a lot of different shots, a lot of variety, and that instead of trying to use one shot more than others, perhaps I should try to use each shot less, to be more unpredictable.

I tried it the next time with a guy who had beaten me a half dozen times in a row, and it worked. I won 6–1 then 6–4, and I had fun doing it. Instead of pressing for winners and berating myself for not hitting the ball as hard as he did, I just took what he gave me and tried to hit the shots that presented themselves. I consciously avoided hitting the same shot twice in a row. It became fun—I was hitting slices, drop shots, moon balls, top spin lobs, and inside-out backhands. It drove him crazy, it took away his rhythm, and it produced unforced errors.

I thought of my son's college basketball coach who was always saying, "Don't force it. Let the game come to you. Don't set up in the same place on the floor every time down the court. Take what the defense gives you." Play with *serendipity!* See what's happening out there, enjoy it, and take advantage of it.

Have a rough game plan going into a match, but be flexible. The tennis definition of serendipity is being aware enough to notice when there is something better than what you planned—little, happy surprises of a new shot that worked or a shallow ball that you can put away or a sudden opportunity to get to the net.

IN LIFE

Horace Walpole, who coined the word *serendipity*, defined it as a state of mind wherein one, through awareness and "sagacity," frequently finds something better than that which he was seeking.

Serendipity is not the absence of plans; it is the ability to be flexible and change plans as situations and circumstances change. It is the ability to notice opportunities or connections and to take advantage of them.

Most great discoveries are serendipitous. Thomas Lennon noticed what happened to rubber when a pot of it boiled over and vulcanized on the stove. Fleming observed some mold that had blown into his laboratory and landed on a petri dish of bacteria—and discovered penicillin.

Each of us, looking back on our lives, can recognize that most of our accomplishments had more to do with spotting an unexpected opportunity than with some detailed, perfectly executed plan.

Have goals and plans, of course, but learn to be observant and flexible enough to notice when something better comes along or where a better, clearer path opens up.

If "stewardship" is the eleven-letter S paradigm that can keep us humble and grateful, then "serendipity" is the other eleven-letter S paradigm that can keep us aware and in tune enough to notice and respond to life's opportunities, beauties, and joys.

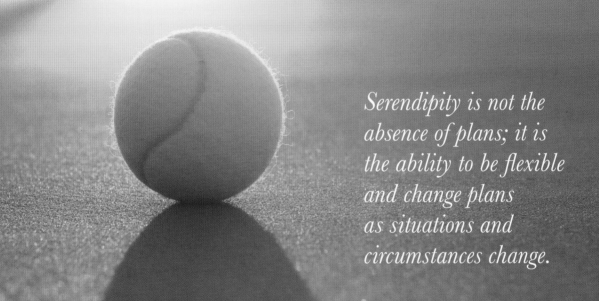

Serendipity is not the absence of plans; it is the ability to be flexible and change plans as situations and circumstances change.

LESSON 20

VISUALIZE
AND FOCUS

IN TENNIS

I was in the media interview room at Roland-Garros, and because of a weekly newspaper column I write, I had press credentials and got to ask a post-match question to Maria Sharapova. "What are you thinking about when you pause at the baseline after each point, face away from the court, and briefly shut your eyes?" She gave a quick answer: "I'm refocusing and visualizing the next point."

She does it after every point. And why not? Why not separate the points from each other in this way and think about the next one for a second before you play it? She also said that her grunt as she hits each stroke (some would say her "shriek") helps her focus on the precise moment of impact.

Rafa Nadal accomplishes the same kind of focus through his little rituals—placing his water bottles in a precise pattern by his chair between games, tugging his shorts, and tucking his hair behind both ears before each point—these are all parts of his way of centering.

Most recreational tennis players have experienced a more subconscious form of visualization: they've been watching Wimbledon or the US Open on Tennis Channel or ESPN2, and when they go out and play later in the day, *violà*—they are hitting their shots better. When you watch Roger Federer hit his gorgeous backhand throughout a televised match, you find that your own stroke starts to imitate it (slightly).

Simply watching the ball is the easiest way to stay focused. Try to watch it so hard that you can see the writing on the ball. Watch it all the way to your racket.

IN LIFE

There are many ways to think yourself into what you want to do and want to be. Benjamin Franklin did it by picking words that described the way he wanted to be and then visualizing himself with those qualities.

A simple way to visualize is to just watch great people. When you expose yourself to greatness, in any field, that greatness becomes more familiar to you, and you begin (even subconsciously) to imitate and incorporate it.

I had been struggling with my first serve, so I got a bucket of balls and went out on the court by myself to see if I could diagnose and fix my problem. After a while, I realized that I was not getting the power or speed I needed from either of the two natural power boosters: shoulder rotation and wrist snap. As I kept serving, I found I could focus on one of the two but then would slack off on the other. Then I tried a little mantra as I served each ball: "Rotate and snap down." Just saying that, out loud or in my mind, seemed to help. On "Rotate," I turned my back more to the net, and on "and snap down," I came around and powered the ball down with a hard wrist snap.

It is amazing how much a little phrase can influence outcomes. And if it can in tennis, it can do it in life. Once I realized that, I did my own rendition of Ben Franklin's self-programming words. My words were perhaps a little more exotic and less practical than his—words like serendipity, stewardship, élan, and pizazz—but I focused on them like he did and rehearsed them through my mind as I ran each morning. Gradually but certainly, thoughts can become reality.

Gradually but certainly, thoughts can become reality.

PLAY YOUR GAME, BUT HAVE MORE THAN ONE GAME

IN TENNIS

Everyone knows the old and true adage "Don't play your opponent's game." If we let the person on the other side of the net dictate the type of points we play, we are doomed. If you are playing against a retrieving rabbit and you play defense with him, he wins because it is his game. If you are playing a big power hitter and you try to outhit him, he overpowers you.

But to play your game is not as simple as not playing his.

Go into a match with a game plan based on what you do well, but then adjust that plan during the warm-up based on what you learn about your opponent's strengths and weaknesses.

And once your plan is adjusted, implement it!

But don't lock on to your plan and ignore the reality of the match. If you see new things, alter your game plan accordingly. You don't have only one game to play. If he is a retriever, you may have to go for more offense and shorten the points. If he is tiring, you want to extend the points.

Have three or four basic games that are all your games, and be able to shift from one to the other as the situation demands. And if you don't think you can, think of Federer who, after sixteen years on the tour, went back and retooled his game with the express purpose of beating Djokovic.

IN LIFE

When I was a small boy, my Swedish grandfather, a carpenter, had me try to cut through a board with a very dull saw. There was lots of sawing but not much result. Then he took his file, sharpened the saw, and had me try again. I will never forget the feeling of sudden efficiency and power as the blade smoothly slid through the wood.

Mental work is often more important than physical work. Planning is often what makes the difference. Most people don't really have life plans; they just live day to day, and that's okay if you just want to float and don't care whether or not you succeed.

But if you're out to make a difference, to maximize yourself and your life, a plan is essential.

Life is unpredictable, so you need flexible, adjustable plans, and you need a Plan B or a Plan C to shift into when Plan A is not working.

The only thing worse than having no plan is having one that isn't working and doggedly sticking with it anyway. Stubbornly clinging to a failing or wrong plan is a predictor of ongoing failure.

Success comes most often to those who have plans but who are willing and capable of adjusting those plans according to circumstance and opportunity. The key is to learn when to stop sawing and pause long enough to sharpen the saw, when to rethink the game you are playing and find a more efficient or more creative way to get to where you want to go.

The only thing worse than having no plan is having one that isn't working and doggedly sticking with it anyway.

LIGHTNING AND WAVES; POWER, TOUCH, AND SPIN

IN TENNIS

No one has to explain to a tennis player how important touch is or how much spin can affect a tennis ball. A player with soft "asbestos" hands is like a magician with the ball—he can take the pace off, dump a drop volley, and flick a half volley down the line. And the masters of spin can swipe up and across a ball to create a top spin lob, stay low and carve down on a slice, or even get around the outside of a ball and hook a drive sideways into the court. No one needs to tell a tennis fan about McEnroe's hands or Rafa's spin.

And despite the general conclusion that today's game is all about power, it is often the finesse and variety—the touch and spin—that makes the difference.

It's like the ball itself works in partnership with the player who has touch and spin. The obedient ball comes alive (or dies) off the racket and seems to devotedly follow the player's will.

But if all you have is touch and spin, you have too few options, and your opponent will adjust.

Add some kind of power—learn to hit flat and drive the ball through the court. Move in on shallow balls and punish them to the open part of the court.

It is the mix of power and speed with touch and spin that makes your game complete. Think of the first as lightning—striking hard and fast—and of the second as waves, flowing and subtle. Develop a game that mirrors two of nature's irresistible forces.

IN LIFE

There seem to be two rather opposite "modes" or mental styles of working that are productive for me. One is when I am relaxed and calm, taking things as they come, enjoying the day and experiencing serendipity. The other is when I am energized and highly efficient, checking things off my to-do list in rapid-fire fashion.

The first mode is like gentle waves—smooth and slow yet strong. The second mode is like lightning—striking bright and fast like a connected series of checkmarks.

Staying too long in the lightning mode is exhausting, and staying in waves day after day can feel a little lazy. Alternating them, juxtaposing them so each makes you aware and appreciative of the other, is the best and most productive way to live.

The waves mode often involves some easy and effective touch and spin. Good negotiators have a magic touch; they are in touch with those they are working with or dealing with and there is a connection made. It might be by actual physical touch—a hand on a shoulder or a touch on a forearm—or it might just be a tasteful, feel-good kind of initiative or response so the receiver feels trusted.

"Spin" gets a bad rap from politics, in which spin doctors try to twist their candidate's words and events to mean what they want them to mean or what voters want to hear. But positive spin can create unity and agreement and can avoid conflict and acrimony.

The lightning mode is all about power and speed and getting a lot done in a little time. It involves goals and lists and check-offs, and when it is well executed, it leaves solid achievement in its wake.

Using a good mix of lightning and waves gives a workday texture and balance.

Using a good mix of lightning and waves gives a workday texture and balance.

TRUST YOUR HANDS; TRUST YOUR BEST STROKE; TRUST YOUR INSTINCTS

IN TENNIS

I take pride in continuing to beat my sons even though they are fitter, stronger, and better athletes than I am. I've got a certain psychological advantage over them, and my game has a lot more variety, countering their athleticism. Each summer I can get through without them beating me is another notch on my pistol handle. I like to think it's keeping me young.

My youngest son (and our best tennis player) gets gratifyingly frustrated as my slices and lobs and drop shots neutralize his power, and he says things like "You don't even move your feet and you hit like a wimp, but your hands save you every time."

And he's right. As you lose the feet, it's the hands that save you. Less foot speed is compensated for by good feel with the hands. Unlike the rest of your body, your hands seem to get better with age. And when you trust your hands, it brings a confidence into the rest of your game so that you trust your instincts and your gut.

Here's an opposite experience: I was playing in the Annual National Hard Court for my age group. I won my first round and played the ninth seed in the second round. I got off to a fairly good start, but my opponent's accuracy was stunning and he was totally consistent. The more games I lost, the more conservative I became, losing trust and slicing every forehand.

After he beat me, his only comment was "You didn't trust your forehand." The comment hurt because my forehand is usually my best weapon and because it was true. But it gave me a new way to think about my game. A forehand is something to trust. You have given a lot of time and effort to it, and it now deserves your trust.

IN LIFE

In life, your forehand might be your professional expertise or your education or your social personality. When you start to doubt any of these, to lose confidence and trust in them, you start pressing and you lose your natural flow.

You have worked hard to become who you are, to learn what you have learned, to be able to do what you do, to instinctively know what has to be done, and to believe that you can do it.

Your hands might be compared to your social skills or your personality or your ability to ask the right question and to listen. Your hands might be your experience—something that gets better and more extensive the longer you live.

Know your resources and your gifts and appreciate them.

Most of all, trust your instincts; trust your gut. After gathering the facts, doing your due diligence, and getting opinions and input from others, most decisions come down to what you feel, and those instincts are usually right.

Doubt is your enemy. Never confuse the asset of humility with the liability of doubt. Be modest, but believe. Trust yourself.

Be modest, but believe.
Trust yourself.

PLAY UP, NOT DOWN

IN TENNIS

There is no mystery in it—we rise or fall to the level of those we play tennis with. Playing down and winning more often may be good for your ego, but it is bad for your game. If you can find players who usually beat you but who are still willing to play, you are on course to up your game.

It's like a little mathematical formula:

Play people you can beat = game deterioration
Play people you are even with = game stagnation
Play people that usually beat you = game improvement

It's not that hard to find and schedule matches with players a bit above you. We often just don't do it because we like winning better than losing. You can get more challenging opponents by entering tournaments and playing in an NTRP level that challenges you or by playing in a tough league. Or you can simply have the courage to get acquainted with better players and set up matches with them.

Once again, it gets back to the question of why you play. If all you want is a bit of exercise and the high you get from winning, play down. But if you play because you want to challenge yourself and become better, play up.

IN LIFE

It's comfortable to be with people who are very similar to you and to stay away from (or at least not seek out) those who challenge you, who see the world differently than you, or who travel in different circles than you.

But the growth and the broadening and the excitement lie in doing the reverse. Of course, you will stay in touch with and work with and socialize with much-in-common friends. But looking for ways to get outside of your social comfort zone more often is what creates a path to a wider perspective and a more interesting social life.

I know one couple who reserves Friday nights to go to dinner with someone new—someone who seems to be coming from a different place, someone who will broaden their view.

The same kind of thinking works in the workplace. Seek out and get to know people who are above you in the corporate structure or who have had professional experience that you might aspire to someday. From their standpoint, it is interesting how compelling and how complimentary it is to be asked for advice or for perspective by someone who looks up to you. Busy and important people will often go out of their way to accommodate you if your request has to do with learning from them, and being asked for advice is a very genuine kind of compliment.

It comes down to why we live. If it's just to tread water and get by, no need to leave the comfort zone, but if life is about progress and growth, keep pushing your zone higher.

*If life is about progress and growth,
keep pushing your zone higher.*

LESSON 25

EXTRACENTEREDNESS

IN TENNIS

I was playing a new friend for the first time, a well-known, highly successful businessman. He seemed strong and confident in the warm-up, and I assumed I was in for a tough match. He served first and reeled off four straight points. I began to wonder if I could even keep it close. But I held my serve, and then in the third game, a surprising thing happened. On deuce, he served a very weak second serve into the net for a double fault. On my ad, he played tentatively. At first, I thought he'd pulled a muscle or something. But as we started the fourth game, he was back to hitting hard. But, again, we got to deuce and again, he went soft and tentative.

How interesting, I thought. *A guy this successful and self-assured in business who clutches on almost every key point.* I began to notice other patterns in his game . . . what shots he would resort to on tough points, how he would berate himself after a miss, and his body language between points.

What I didn't notice right at the time but realized later was how well I was playing. I was so absorbed in watching him, analyzing his play, trying to guess what he was thinking, that I was completely unconscious of my own game and was playing instinctively, moving easily to the ball, hitting hard and clean and well. I had become so fascinated with what was going on in his mind that it had cleared my own.

In tennis, too much self-awareness is a killer. If you think too hard about a stroke, it goes south! Too much analysis creates paralysis. And a good way to get your mind off of yourself is to focus on your opponent.

IN LIFE

In life, there are two simple reasons for wanting and trying to be extracentered (that is, focused on others, on the external, and on the principles or attitudes you want to live by) rather than self-centered. One is that it allows you to appreciate more, to help more, to be a better spouse, a better parent, and a better friend. The other is that it takes your mind off yourself, lessens stress and self-consciousness, and allows you to be your better, more natural, more spontaneous self.

"Being a force of Nature," is how George Bernard Shaw phrased it, "instead of a feverish selfish little clod of ailments and grievances complaining that the world will not devote itself to making you happy."

In tennis, the worst way to stop thinking about your forehand is to tell yourself to quit thinking about your forehand. In life, the way to be less self-conscious and self-absorbed is *not* to tell yourself to quit thinking about yourself but to think and focus on something else . . . preferably on another person that you care about.

"Love of our neighbour," George MacDonald wrote, "is the only door out of the dungeon of self."[6]

There are, of course, times to focus and think very hard about yourself—to be introspective, self-critical, and analytical. In tennis, it's best to think about your strokes when you practice but not when you play. In life, think about yourself—your goals, your skills, your faults, your progress or lack of it—when you *plan*, when you are alone within yourself and working on the questions of who you are and where you are going.

But when you are with other people, think about *them*, and your empathy will clear and free you from your self-doubts even as it understands and helps those you care about.

When you are with other people, think about them, and your empathy will clear and free you from your self-doubts.

DOUBLES

LESSON 26

COMMITMENT

We've all been in matches that were won or lost simply because one player wanted it more than the other—was more committed to winning. Being committed to a match is something that energizes you and spurs the extra effort—and it is something an opponent can see and feel.

But there is another kind of commitment that is equally powerful, and it applies in doubles. The worst doubles mindset is to be playing with a partner who you feel is evaluating you, critiquing you, and deciding whether he wants to continue to play with you. You feel like you are on trial or in an interview or a test, like your partner wishes you would do things differently, blames points lost on you, and keeps waiting for you to lift your game up to his expectations.

A critical, judgmental doubles partner is as bad as it gets. But the opposite is as good as it gets. When you have an encouraging partner, one who seems to approve of everything you do, one that acts like he is lucky to play with you, life is good—and your game gets better!

Be that kind of a doubles partner! Let the other person on your side of the net see that you are all in, that you believe in him or her, that you are committed! Mistakes are okay—you are in it for the long haul. You give your partner real security with this total commitment, and you may find that, ironically, you have more influence and more control over your partner's game than you do over your own.

IN LIFE

If you wanted to put the problems of the world into one word, to describe the one thing we have lost that may be causing us to lose everything, you might choose the word *commitment*.

We live in a time when people, particularly the millennial generation, are avoiding commitment like the plague, especially the commitment of marriage. They are looking for ways to "keep all options open" and to avoid personal and family responsibility.

And it's not working. As columnist and commentator David Brooks says: "People are not better off when they are given maximum personal freedom to do what they want. They're better off when they are enshrouded in commitments that transcend personal choice—commitments to family, God, craft and country."[7]

If you want to give the greatest double gift—to yourself and to the person you love the most—give the gift of total commitment. It is the gift that keeps on giving. It gives security and confidence; it gives tolerance and the chance to start over; it gives an unconditional love that can free your partner from guilt and stress and doubt.

There is a fundamental misunderstanding in our society today about what commitment is and when it comes. Couples cohabitate with the reasoning that they are trying out living together and if it works, they will make the commitment of marriage. After all, "you wouldn't buy a car until you had given it a test drive." But here is the problem: when hard times or serious disagreements come, it is commitment that gets you through them. Commitment is the beginning of a live-together relationship, not the culmination of it. In life as well as in tennis doubles, it is commitment that allows you to play your best game.

In life as well as in tennis doubles, it is commitment that allows you to play your best game.

FIND THE ANGLES

IN TENNIS

Singles, they say, is a game of power, while doubles is a game of angles.
There is so much more to the court than we usually use. If you diagram the ball paths in a typical match, it is amazing how the majority of shots are within a few degrees of the straight length of the court. Most shots, particularly on shallow balls hit from inside the baseline, could be angled by another thirty or forty degrees and still land "in."

I used to play singles with a friend who had been a nationally ranked doubles player and who could also be a bit of a trash talker. "Let me introduce you to some parts of the court you haven't met," he would say. And he often did—not only on sharply angled volleys but also with shots from the baseline that landed both shallower and closer to the sideline than I was used to. I felt like I was on a string, jerked back and forth and playing half of the match racing to hit balls that were so sharply angled that I had to run out of the court to get them.

We call it "finding an angle," and that is just what it is—sensing the spot in the opponent's court where the angle (and the distance he has to travel) is maximized.

In doubles, of course, those opportunities are magnified. The extra five feet of the doubles alley allows angles to increase by major proportions, and forty-five-degree-plus angles on groundstrokes can be common. And great doubles players angle some of their close-to-net volleys at almost ninety degrees!

Finding angles is a product of looking for them and practicing them until the fear of hitting wide is replaced by the love and anticipation of hitting sharp, angled winners.

IN LIFE

So much of success in today's world lies in finding a new way to do something, seeing a new need, grasping a new perspective, or discovering a new *angle*.

Doing everything the accepted, standard way is like hitting the ball down the center of the court every time. The alternative of looking constantly for angles and shortcuts and new paths is what generates progress (not to mention profits).

Some call it "thinking out of the box" or "an outlier mentality." But whatever it is called, the ability to look for and find new approaches and new angles may be the most valuable skill there is in our rapid-change world.

As in tennis, a couple—or a team—has greater opportunities for finding angles than a single person who essentially has a "smaller court."

In good marriages, the goal is not to see how similar two people can be but rather to see how synergistically the unique skills of each can be brought together and used in a complementary way to produce more efficiency and greater potential.

Like the added width of a doubles court in tennis, the greater breadth of a married couple working in tandem and in teamwork opens up more opportunities and better angles.

Like the added width of a doubles court in tennis, the greater breadth of a married couple working in tandem and in teamwork opens up more opportunities and better angles.

SYNERGICITY, SPECIALIZATION, AND ONENESS

IN TENNIS

Identical, mirror-image twins come from the same egg and develop facing each other within the womb. They are exactly alike but backwards or reversed from each other. One twin is left handed, one right; one has a crown-of-head cowlick that goes clockwise, and the other's goes counterclockwise.

In the case of the Bryan brothers, it made for the perfect doubles team. It seems that everything one of them does complements and balances what the other one does.

While most of us are not twins with our doubles partners, we can strive for the same kind of complementary specialization. Put your better forehand on the forehand side. Have your better server serve first every set. If there is a lob in the center of the court, let the partner with the best overhead take it.

Equality does not mean sameness. The fact that you are equal doubles partners does not mean that you both have to do the same things with the same proficiency. Specialize wherever the game allows. You become one in a coordinated and unified game, not by cloning each other but by developing complementing and compensating sets of skills.

Synergy means a situation (or a doubles team) in which the total is greater than the sum of its parts. Synchronicity means meshing in a way that is natural and timely and mutually beneficial. Combining the word can create a new word that is the perfect description of how a good doubles team plays or performs—"synergicity."

Focusing on and developing synergicity can lead to a kind of oneness in which a doubles team becomes a single organism, functioning together, as one, to achieve the desired end of winning.

IN LIFE

One of the major misconceptions in many marriages is thinking that equality means sameness. This takes the form of couples who think that in order to be equal, they have to each work the same number of hours, each change the baby's diaper an equal number of times, each take fifty percent of every role, duty, and responsibility.

This is nonsense, of course. To make a business comparison, it would be like saying, "The vice president of marketing has to do exactly what the vice president of production does or they are not equal."

Couples trying to share every role and function equally are forcing a kind of unnatural equality that rarely works. On the other hand, couples who appreciate each other's different abilities and attributes and who learn to specialize and synergize around those differences seem to find a natural synchronicity built on teamwork and mutual admiration and respect.

Irrespective of gender, if one partner is the more natural nurturer while the other is more inclined and suited for the workplace, the professions pursued and the functionality of the marriage should be structured to maximize those differing skills and inclinations.

Another business analogy would be two "limited partnerships," one for the "inner" aspects of home and children and one for the "outer" functions of work or financial maintenance. Both partners would do things in both worlds and have equal ownership and vesting in each of the two partnerships, but one would be the "general partner" in each, keeping the other partner fully versed and involved. A merged oneness of maximized strengths would be the result.

Couples who appreciate each other's different abilities and attributes and who learn to specialize and synergize around those differences seem to find a natural synchronicity built on teamwork and mutual admiration and respect.

CREATE EACH OTHER

IN TENNIS

"I want to be a better doubles player, so I had better start changing my partner."

As ridiculous as that sounds, it is often the way we think. "If he would just get his first serve in more." "Why can't he cover his alley?" Unspoken criticism can be felt, and it has a profoundly negative effect on how your partner plays and on how you do as a team.

Of course, if you want to be a better doubles player, it is yourself you need to work on.

But instead of thinking individually, if you change your thinking a bit and think collectively in terms of becoming a better doubles *team*, it opens up some positive possibilities for improving your two individual games in the process.

The principle involved is that people tend to live up to their reputation. If you give your partner a reputation of consistency, he will become more consistent. If he knows you think he volleys well under pressure, he will do it. Through compliments, encouragement, accolades, and affirmation, you can give your partner a positive reputation that will reflect more and more in his actual game.

In fact, and this is the interesting thing, it may be that you have more control over your partner's reputation and self-image than you do over your own. Giving yourself compliments or using positive self-talk may help your own game, but your compliments to your partner may be able, in some ways, to do more for his game than for your own.

When you expect your partner to succeed, to come through, to elevate on the big points, he actually does it, and the mutual confidence (because it is almost always returned) will lift your performance as a doubles team more than anything else you can do.

IN LIFE

"I want to be a better parent, so I need to start changing my kids."
"I want to have a better marriage, so I need to start changing my spouse."

It is comically wrong thinking, but it happens all the time. And, of course, we actually become better husbands or wives or parents only by working on ourselves.

But there is a caveat to that: our partners can make us better (or worse) at these roles by the kind of reputation they give us. The way your partner sees you and what you can do in their eyes has a profound effect on what you actually can do.

There is so much criticism and negative messaging going on in marriages. A disgusted look, a sharp word, a "there you go again" attitude can wear a partner down and undermine her confidence and enthusiasm while encouragement, approval, and straight-up, in-the-eye compliments can actually change how she perceives herself and change, in turn, how well she does things and how she feels about herself.

It's fine to try to self-talk and have a positive mental attitude in order to make yourself feel more capable and confident, but research shows that someone else saying it to you has more credibility than you saying it to yourself, which means that we have more control over how our spouse feels, over how confident she is, over how she feels about herself than we do over those feelings in ourselves. The same applies with our children.

By focusing on the positive, by genuinely appreciating, by looking for opportunities to compliment, we literally begin to create our partner and our children and to impact their happiness.

By focusing on the positive, by genuinely appreciating, by looking for opportunities to compliment, we literally begin to create our partner and our children and to impact their happiness.

COMMUNICATION

IN TENNIS

It's true in all sports: "Talk on defense!" My high school basketball coach used to scream at us, "Communicate! Let your teammates know where you are!"

Communication between doubles partners may be the most essential of all. If you don't know where he will be on the court, it's likely you yourself will be in the wrong spot. You need to know if he is going to poach, if he is going to follow his serve in, if he is hitting the spin serve or the flat one.

Tennis doubles communication happens in two ways. The first is through signals or actual talk about where you will be or what you will do on the next shot. The second is just knowing your partner well enough that you sense what shot he will hit from certain parts of the court or what kind of approach shots he likes to follow in to the net.

Generally speaking, though, there are five things that have to be well and constantly communicated between doubles partners:

1. Your general strategy for a particular match
2. Which of your two opponents you will hit to in equal situations
3. Where you are each going to be on the court
4. When you are going to poach or switch sides of the court
5. Where you will hit your second serve

Being on the same page on these five is the key to better doubles and more wins. And since every match is different, it's not enough to have one single formula for any of the five. The communication has to be ongoing and up to date.

IN LIFE

If you were to ask one hundred married couples what the key element in a good spousal relationship is, ninety-five of them would probably say "communication."

But what does that overused word really mean in a marriage partnership? Does it mean having no secrets from each other? Does it mean openness—being transparent in how you feel? Does it mean sharing details about your daily life and activities? Does it mean setting goals and planning together? Does it mean asking each other questions and knowing where you each are coming from on issues big and small? Does it mean all of the above?

Most importantly, does marital communication just happen or does there need to be a deliberate and conscious effort to communicate? And if so, what about?

Interestingly, the five most common reasons given for divorce can also be thought of as the five things couples need to communicate constantly and effectively about if they want to stay together. The five are:

1. Goals and aspirations
2. Beliefs and convictions
3. Sex and intimacy
4. Children and parenting
5. Money and finances

Assuming that you agree on these things is not enough, nor is talking about them once in a while. Each is a fluid thing that evolves and changes over time, and communicating about each of them deliberately and consistently is what deepens and equalizes partnerships and keeps marriages on track—on an upward track.

Communication is what deepens and equalizes partnerships and keeps marriages on track.

AFTER MATCH AND AFTERMATH:

A Simple Suggestion for Implementation

Implementation by Conscious Concentration and by Subconscious Self-Programming

Lesson 20 referenced Benjamin Franklin's systematic method for self-improvement, and a little expansion of that type of thinking may be the best and most reliable way to approach the "putting into practice" of all of the perspectives of this book.

Now Ben, to my knowledge, didn't play tennis. (He sure wasn't built for it.) He did, however, have a pretty great system for *implementing* or incorporating into his life the principles or characteristics he had chosen for himself. Essentially, he would identify a quality he desired (like punctuality or self-discipline) and focus on making that trait a part of everything he did for a week. The next week, he'd concentrate on another desired quality. It could be thought of as the "B. F. Program for Step-by-Step Implementation."

Based on that model, here is a conscious application plan for the thirty perspectives or principles of this book: pick a couple of the perspectives that you feel like you need and go out on the court (or out into life) with them firmly in mind. Make those two perspectives your focus during the next two-week period (a "fortnight," as the British say—and the length of Wimbledon and the other majors). Then, during that fortnight, try to center every tennis match you play on the two chapters you have chosen. At the same time, center your everyday life on those same chapters during those same two weeks.

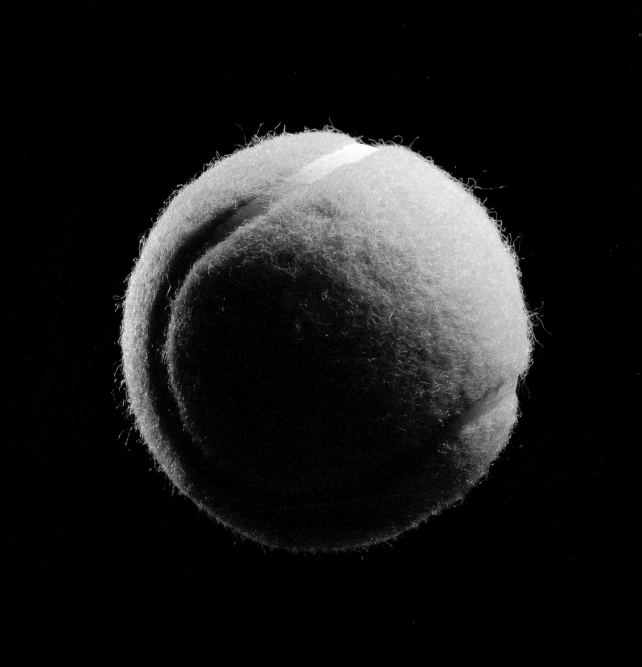

At the end of the fortnight, shift your focus to another pair of perspectives that you think work well together. Then, as time passes, keep at it, piece by piece, perspective by perspective, until you have tried them all. Then repeat them . . . rotate them . . . find your favorites . . . add your own. Make both tennis and life thinking games.

Socrates said that the unexamined life was not worth living. Similarly, the unexamined tennis game is not worth playing.

After a time—less time than you might think—the perspectives will begin to be *part* of you . . . part of your tennis game . . . part of your life. You will begin to apply them subconsciously. And your application of a perspective in tennis will make you more aware of your use of that same perspective in your life.

And you will start winning both games more often.

The key is getting the perspectives firmly into your subconscious mind. Once they are embedded there, they begin to work automatically and consistently, both in the way we play tennis and in the way we live life. Once a principle or perspective is in your subconscious—once it's a part of your inner mental and emotional makeup—you begin to follow it and do it naturally, automatically, and without conscious thought; just as a tennis stroke, once it is in your "muscle memory," it will happen naturally and automatically.

Besides the two-per-fortnight conscious concentration, there is a second way to input the perspectives into your subconscious. And we really need two separate approaches because each of the perspectives needs to be individually downloaded into your head over and over until it becomes a part of you.

So the second absorption method is this: pick some activity you do very routinely and very regularly—daily running or showering or shaving—and during that running time or shower time or whatever routine activity you have chosen, mentally scroll through as many of the perspectives as you can remember. Call them up, by title, one by one in your mind. Use the Table of Contents as a cheat sheet if you have to. When you come to one that is vague to you, re-read that chapter.

While you are running or exercising or shaving or showering for the betterment of your body, be self-programming the perspectives for the betterment of your brain. Think of the perspectives as *your* characteristics, as *descriptions* of how you play both games, as part of who you are. You have adopted these qualities, they are yours, and you *are* them. Say to yourself, "I start strong" and give yourself positive feedback by thinking of specific times when you did start strong—in tennis or in a life situation. Then say, "I play with serendipity" and think of points or instances in which you saw and took an unexpected opportunity. Say, "I break back" and back it up by thinking of times when you showed resilience on the court or in your life.

Don't think of the perspectives as what you want to have or what you wish to be; think of them as already part of you. They are! They became a part of you the moment you decided on them and mentally adopted them. Now you are reinforcing them and confirming their inclusion in your self-image.

Programming yourself in this way embeds the perspectives in your subconscious.

Gradually, more and more, as time goes by and as you program them in over and over, you will experience the joy of feeling them, of doing them, of implementing them naturally, without conscious thought or effort on the court and in the day to day.

And, as a bonus, shaving or running or the StairMaster or the treadmill or whatever routine activity you use for your self-programming will become less boring!

Bottom line: combine. Combine body conditioning and mind conditioning and let each complement the other. Combine the perspectives of tennis with the perspectives of life and let each influence and enhance the other. Combine your love of tennis with your love of life and learn to play both games better and longer.

Love life! Love tennis!

Endnotes

1. Lee, Harold B. *Strengthening the Home*. Salt Lake City, Utah: The Church of Jesus Christ of Latter-day Saints, 1973. P. 7.

2. McKay, David O. *Conference Report, April 1964*. Salt Lake City, Utah: The Church of Jesus Christ of Latter-day Saints, 1964. P. 5.

3. Eyre, Richard and Linda. *The Entitlement Trap: How to Rescue Your Child with a New Family System of Choosing, Earning, and Ownership*. New York: Penguin Group, 2011.

4. Carlson, Richard. *Don't Sweat the Small Stuff . . . and It's All Small Stuff*. New York: Hyperion, 1997.

5. Chesterton, G. K. *Orthodoxy*. New York: John Lane Company, 1908.

6. MacDonald, George. *Epea Aptera: Unspoken Sermons*. London: Alexander Strahan, 1867.

7. Brooks, David. "The Age of Possibility." *New York Times*, November 15, 2012, http://www.nytimes.com/2012/11/16/opinion/brooks-the-age-of-possibility.html?_r=1.

About the Author

RICHARD EYRE'S writing spans the lifestyle and self-improvement spectrum from diet and health to work/life balance to marriage and parenting. Often coauthoring with his wife, Linda, his books have sold in the millions and been translated into more than a dozen languages. The Eyres' most recent books are *Life in Full, The Turning, The Thankful Heart,* and *The Half-Diet Diet.* For a full list, visit www.EyresFreeBooks.com.

Richard was a Harvard Business School–trained management and political consultant until his first bestseller changed his career to full-time author and speaker (and part-time tennis player). The Eyres have nine children and twenty-eight grandchildren and are relishing the "autumn" of their lives. They lecture throughout the world (forty-five countries and counting) on their books and on the programs and paradigms on their websites: ValuesParenting.com, TheEyres.com, and Eyrealm.com.

In tennis, Richard is winning a war of attrition—each time he moves into a higher age category, he goes up in the rankings because a few more of the players who can beat him have retired or quit playing . . . or died.

About Familius

Welcome to a place where mothers and fathers are celebrated, not belittled. Where values are at the core of happy family life. Where boo-boos are still kissed, cake beaters are still licked, and mistakes are still okay. Welcome to a place where books—and family—are beautiful. Familius: a book publisher dedicated to helping families be happy.

If you feel a few friends and family might benefit from what you've read, let us know and we'll be happy to provide you with quantity discounts. Simply email us at orders@familius.com.

Website: www.familius.com
Facebook: www.facebook.com/paterfamilius
Twitter: @familiustalk, @paterfamilius1
Pinterest: www.pinterest.com/familius

FAMILIUS

The most important work you ever do will be within the walls of your own home.